Tyneside's Finest

The Half Moon Inn, Bigg Market, Newcastle, around 1910.

Tyneside's Finest

a miscellany

Tyne Bridge Publishing

Acknowledgements

Tyne Bridge Publishing, the publishing arm of Newcastle Libraries, would like to give hearty thanks to all our contributors for their hard work and patience. We must thank John Grundy in particular for his preface.

This book was never intended to be a comprehensive appreciation of Tyneside. It is a rather a miscellany of personal opinions and topics dear to the hearts of writers and local historians with a connection to Tyne Bridge Publishing, and Newcastle Libraries. It is therefore unashamedly biased, partisan and selective and we apologise in advance for omissions.

We do hope you will enjoy reading it as much as we have enjoyed bringing it together.

We would also like to thank, in our biased opinion, Tyneside's finest printer, Elanders Hindson, who have been immensely supportive throughout this venture. Our gratitude also to Hay's Binding Solutions, and to Donald Murray Paper Co.

Illustrations are from the collections of Newcastle Libraries unless otherwise indicated. Many thanks to photographers Samantha Fairless (SF), and Thomas Yellowley (TY).

Cover design: Anthony Flowers.
Frontispiece photograph: Justice, from the old County Court *(Thomas Yellowley)*.

©Tyne Bridge Publishing, 2006

ISBN: 185795 109 3
978 185795 109 7

Published by City of Newcastle upon Tyne
Newcastle Libraries & Information Service,
Tyne Bridge Publishing, 2006
www.tynebridgepublishing.co.uk

Binding produced by Hay's Binding Solutions, Newcastle upon Tyne
Paper provided by Donald Murray Paper Co.

Printed by Elanders Hindson, North Tyneside

Contents

Tyneside's finest things

Fishing boats off the Tyne around 1890, from Newcastle Libraries Local Studies photographic collection.

A remarkable place

What a remarkable place Tyneside is ...

The briefest glance at the chapter headings in this book will reveal to you at least two quite distinct things about it. It will reveal to you first of all that Geordies are an odd lot; that if you give fifty or so interesting Tynesiders the opportunity to write about a Tyneside topic of their choice they come up with an extraordinary range of people, places and things. I bet that when they first thought about the book, the publishers had no idea that the eventual list would be so varied – but I bet they're glad it is. There are lots of things here and lots of people that I'd never heard of, I bet there are lots that you haven't either – but as soon as I saw the list I wanted to find out about them ...

But the list also reveals that Tyneside is, and always has been, a remarkable place, quite different from anywhere else in the country. What a range there is here. There's great architecture of course; we on Tyneside are rich in great architecture but we've always been proud to find riches in our back streets too. There's industry and entertainment, philosophy, crime, culture, drink. There are things that are intensely local and there are others – works of engineering brilliance for example – which have played a part in transforming the whole world. And then there are the people – as bizarre a range as you'd find on the last Metro home on a Saturday night – and that's saying something. There are lots of good people who made a difference to the world and a few bad ones too. There are geniuses and madmen – and some who were undoubtedly both.

This book is like a kaleidoscope. The history of Tyneside, its experience, influence, greatness and variety is presented as a picture made up of more than a hundred little fragments. That's what kaleidoscopes are, of course, but this one is unusual because each individual fragment is a story in its own right, each one is sharply focused and passionate and opinionated. As a result, what emerges from the book as a whole isn't a picture of Tyneside like a tourist brochure would provide – all pretty and historical and predictable – but it is a picture which you'll recognise if you come from here; and if you don't already know Tyneside you can take it from me that 'Tyneside's Finest ...' provides a pretty accurate picture of one of the finest places in Britain.

John Grundy, 2006

Coming home

Geordies are great travellers. You can go almost anywhere in the world and meet a fellow Tynesider. Most of them, however, always feel a connection with the North East and can usually describe a special view that they always associate with coming home.

The return to the Tyne

Coming home! The heart of many a seaman and passenger must have been lifted up when the ship rounded the Tyne piers and the safety of the harbour beckoned. From the 18th century the High and Low Lights indicated the right line to steer avoiding the twin hazards of the Black Middens and the Herd Sands.

They were not the only dangers encountered by voyagers entering the mouth of the Tyne. There was also Jingling Geordie, who lit a fire in the mouth of his cave in the cliff below Knotts Flats. His aim was to confuse the pilot and cause a wreck. Then he could take his pick of the cargoes and personal items washed ashore. His legend was still being told in the 1930s.

Constance Fraser

Newcastle c.1880. The final destination of many ships entering the Tyne.

Hastings' Auty Series, Whitley Bay.

Low Lights, North Shields.

The Low Lights at North Shields with the mouth of the Tyne beyond, around 1900.

Lighting the way home

Completed in 1808, the lights were first lit in the lanterns of the High and Low Lights on 1 May 1810. Standing tall, one above the other, they are the Tyne's leading marks. Keep them in transit and they will guide you safely into Shields Harbour, clear of the Rock End, the Black Middens, Prior's Stone and the Herd Sand – local hazards which mark the watery graves of many ships and men. The present lights replaced an earlier pair built in 1727.

Richard E. Keys

The view from the train

For Tynesiders surely the finest view is that enjoyed by homecoming Geordies travelling from the south by train. Visitors, or voyagers travelling onward into Scotland, must be astonished when they see this breathtaking view for the first time. Often the train has to stop on the King Edward VII Bridge to await a vacant platform in the Central Station, giving passengers time to appreciate the view from the bridge.

Looking east from the train you see the broad sweep of the River

Tyne flowing to the North Sea and the magnificent array of bridges crossing the river to link Newcastle with its neighbour, Gateshead. Other cities have bridges, some, like London, many more bridges than here, but they have nothing compared to our view. First there is the Queen Elizabeth II (Metro) Bridge and then the engineering triumph of Robert Stephenson's High Level Bridge. Further downstream, the technical ingenuity of Lord Armstrong is displayed in the squat, but beautiful, Swing Bridge. Next comes the symbol of home to all exiled Geordies – the Tyne Bridge. Finally, the most recent of all the bridges, the Gateshead Millennium Bridge, winner of so many architectural awards (and justly so) elegantly curves over the river. Look upstream for a view of one more modern bridge, the Redheugh, as the Tyne curves away towards Scotswood and the west.

This is a truly magnificent view, particularly in bright sunshine, and a splendid introduction to Tyneside for visitors travelling by train.

Douglas Bond

North East England possesses two of the finest views in the world to inspire the first time visitor. In both cases you need to travel by train. The first is on Wearside (if you will forgive my mentioning it). As the train sweeps into Durham's high level station you are confronted by the magnificent view across the valley of Durham Cathedral and Castle. I doubt if St Cuthbert's monks had the view in mind when they chose the site but you would go a very long way to beat it.

I would never suggest that Tyneside's finest view (in my opinion) is a rival or it is any way better or worse. Each, in its own way, does the same job.

Travelling from the south, as your train sweeps round the curve in Gateshead and the train begins to cross the Tyne, you can see the spectacular Tyneside bridgescape, equalled nowhere in the world.

The Tyne at this point originally had one bridge. The crossing place was first identified by the Romans – or at least named by them. (I am sure the locals knew where to cross the river even if their engineering skills weren't up to Roman standards). As wheels (both road and rail) began to take over from feet (human and animal) as a means of transport, bridges proliferated. There might have been even more. If the many proposed Tyne crossings had all been built they could have

A train steams south across the High Level Bridge towards Gateshead, around 1970.

obscured the river completely.

Each has idiosyncrasies. The Swing Bridge was built on the site of the Roman and medieval crossings so that the ships could get up river to the shipyards at Elswick (an arch of the medieval bridge can still be seen in a riverside cellar). The High Level – the first cast iron bridge in the world – designed by Stephenson to carry rail and road traffic, was opened by Queen Victoria crossing it in the Royal train. Possibly this was the only time she had a good look at Tyneside, as a dispute with the Royal Station Hotel over a bill caused her to order the curtains to be closed every time she passed through Newcastle in later times (see page 74 for a different version of this story).

The Tyne Bridge, is NOT the model for the Sydney Harbour Bridge. At one time it had the dubious distinction of being the worst traffic bottle neck in Europe. The most recent is the Gateshead Millennium Bridge, which eschews the modern predilection for wheels (except cycles) and is a pedestrian bridge.

Barbara Stephenson

Travels and Travails

Danger and bad weather have never been serious obstacles for Geordie travellers. When they leave the Tyne however, they always look forward to the return journey.

A Voyage in the Coal Trade: Tyneside's finest maritime poem

*A*Voyage in the Coal Trade* (published 1842) concerns a (dramatic) trip away from the Tyne and home again; a journey frequently taken by sailors on colliers and other shipping. If you'd like to read the whole 103 (yes 103!) verses of the ballad there is a copy in Newcastle Libraries' Local Studies collection.

To be honest, there is not too much competition for the title of Tyneside's finest maritime poem (or ballad): the haunting, Nelsonian press-gang images of *The Tender's Coming*; the self-deprecating wonder of Robert Gilchrist's (ship-borne) *Voyage to Lunnin*; and a variety of verses poking fun at that muscle-bound butt, the Keelman. What seems to be lacking in all these though is a big theme, by a big poet. Never fear, *A Voyage in the Coal Trade* has both. For there is no bigger theme than the economic driver of Tyneside's wealth, the carrying of 'coals from Newcastle'. And there is no bigger poet in local anthologies than 'Anon'.

What then, the intending reader may say, of this poem's style and substance? Well, although our anonymous author's verses sometimes tumble about as unpredictably as the waves themselves, he sticks (as near as his vocabulary will allow) to a grand old favourite, a ballad metre, rhyming:

DESCRIPTION

OF

A VOYAGE

IN THE

COAL TRADE;

AN ADDRESS TO SEAMEN,

ESPECIALLY THE RISING YOUTH;

WITH

VALUABLE INFORMATION

TO

MERCHANT SEAMEN.

PRINTED AND SOLD BY W. & T. FORDYCE,
[47] 15, GREY STREET, NEWCASTLE.

Coal brigs off the Gateshead shore around 1890.

a,a,b,b. You'll soon get the idea …

> *All sails now set the breeze to catch,*
> *We clear the decks and set the watch;*
> *One half on deck the watch to keep,*
> *The other half below in hammocks sleep.*

As to substance, the entire 103 verses of the poem are taken up in describing a 'London Voyage' during the early 19th century's heyday of sail – carrying coal from the Tyne to the Thames. How exceedingly boring you might think, but, like a great novel, the narrative exposes many aspects of men's lives and their enduring weaknesses: the vain and overbearing captain; a competent but long suffering first mate, with an unsatisfied appetite (for beef); the gangs of avaricious, bribe-taking, metropolitan officials who frustrate the ship's unloading; a cheating Thameside ballastman, and an agreeable but inebriate water-man –

Shipping at the Mouth of the Tyne, 1845, by John Scott (detail).

> *His name is Sam; a clever fellow,*
> *But Sam sometimes gets a little mellow.*
> *But that you know is nothing new,*
> *For clever fellows often do.*

Finally, bad weather and scant supplies of food and tobacco bedevil the crew's return to the Tyne until, eventually, the familiar landmarks heave into sight and the (now) dismissed mate can console himself with –

> *Well, I'm thankful now we're here at last,*
> *At Fairless' Crane [South Shields] we made her fast;*
> *and will be there I make no doubt,*
> *Until the ballast is all out.*

> *When that will be I need not mind,*
> *Another ship I must try to find:*
> *To-morrow the wages will be paid,*
> *and I'll bid adieu to the COAL TRADE!*

The irony is that he, and other 'common seamen', could never afford to bid such an adieu. Which of us then dare deny them their (and their poem's) place among Tyneside's finest? For, In sunshine days and stormy neets they were, truly, Lords upon the Ocean.

Adrian Osler

Sometimes even the best laid plans go awry ...

Tyneside's most memorable railway opening

Work on the construction of the Newcastle and Carlisle Railway (N&CR) began in 1830 and the line was opened in sections from 1835 onwards. To speed up completion, up to 1400 men were employed on the building of the final phase, between Haydon Bridge and Blenkinsopp. On 18 June 1838, the anniversary of the battle of Waterloo, the official opening of the full length of track took place. As Tomlinson, the author of the stupendous compendium, *The North Eastern Railway*, wrote, it was 'a ceremonial display unequalled perhaps in the history of railways'.

The day began early with five trains leaving Carlisle for Newcastle, where the invited guests were being entertained to a prolonged breakfast in Newcastle's Assembly Rooms. The great journey to Carlisle began in some confusion at 12.30pm, some 90 minutes later than planned, and then the total complement of 3,500 participants was transported the 61 miles to Carlisle in 13 (or 14) trains, many of them in open carriages (some of the dignitaries had to travel in a pig cart as all the reserved carriages had been filled). It rained solidly. The last train did not arrive in Carlisle until 6pm, an hour after it had been due

Trains on the Newcastle & Carlisle Railway at Redheugh Station, Gateshead.

OPENING

OF THE

NEWCASTLE AND CARLISLE

RAILWAY,

On the 18th Instant.

━━━━━━━━◄◄◄◄◄◄◄‹‹‹◦››››››››►━━━━━━━━

NOTICE IS HEREBY GIVEN,

THAT

The MAIN Procession of Trains to CARLISLE,

Will leave the Redheugh Station at 11 o'Clock in the Morning.

No Person can be allowed to enter the Station, or be admitted to the Trains, without a Ticket, on any Pretence whatever; and the Entrances to the Station, both by Land and Water, will be closed at 15 Minutes *before* 11 o'Clock precisely, (in order to allow Time for the necessary Arrangements) after which Time no Person can be admitted.

The Trains will proceed to the *Canal Basin*, CARLISLE, where Parties may leave to obtain Refreshments in the Town. But the Trains, on their *Return to Newcastle*, will depart from the *London Road Station*, Carlisle, at 5 o'Clock precisely.

** No Person can be allowed to go upon the Engines or Tender.

Newcastle and Carlisle Railway Office,
June 11th, 1838.

to set off on the return journey to Newcastle. After a disorderly stampede for refreshments which took the place of a planned procession into the town, the final leg of the journey back to Newcastle did not begin until 10pm.

After a thunderstorm which soaked the guests, some of them only lightly dressed, and a collision and derailment which resulted in injury and inevitable delay, the last train did not arrive in Newcastle until 6am, by which time, it was reported, crowds at the terminus anxiously awaited news of the delayed party.

The chaos was such that the event was very fully covered by the local press, although the details varied slightly between reports. Richard Lowry, an employee of the N&CR wrote in his voluminous diary: 'It has been a dreadful opening to require a whole day and a night to complete it.' In spite of the mishaps, or mismanagement, the N&CR continued for some years to commemorate the anniversary of Waterloo by the firing of a canon but is not clear whether this was done to celebrate the railway's opening or as a patriotic gesture.

Robert W. Rennison

The No. 1 bus

Sights to be seen from the No. 1 bus.

Most large towns have a key bus route that traverses their urban sprawl from end to end; lengthier and more essentially arterial that lesser suburban services, they are the red blood cells of metropolitan life, linking the heart of the city to the furthest reaches of its fingertips. In Newcastle, this service is the appropriately designated No. 1.

As a Heaton resident, the No. 1 is something of a taxi service for me. Early morning journeys to work, weekend shopping expeditions to Northumberland Street, evenings out at the Theatre Royal, and late rides home after a night on the town have all began and ended on these double-decked leviathans that ply our streets at ten-minute intervals from dawn to midnight.

Like all shifts of perspective, seeing familiar streets going by from the upper deck of a bus offers new facets of the passing scenery, invisible to the pedestrians below; the city roofscape as seen from the approach to Heaton Road; eye-to-eye contact with the golden fairy on the Northern Goldsmith's clock; the sweeping views of the winding Tyne as you climb the steep banks to the west of Scotswood.

Twenty-five years ago, the upper deck on an early weekday morning would be full to the gunnels with cloth-capped men and head-scarved women among a sea of newspapers, the air a fug of cigarette smoke, which would clear as if by magic as the bus emptied at the Central Station. Nowadays, not quite so early in the morning, it's filled with students from Coach Lane campus and the warren of Tyneside flats in Heaton and empties much earlier in the University quarter of St Mary's Place. The only caps these days are of the baseball variety, the only cigarette a few rebellious wisps from some defiant teenagers encamped noisily in the back seats.

Changing travel habits and the advent of the Metro have made buses something of a poor relation today. But

A bus crew, 1948.

have you ever seen visitors from other countries, where double deckers are unknown, make straight for the front seat upstairs, and enjoy the ride with finger pointing delight? It happens – and long may it continue to do so. Until, that is, the No. 1 inevitably disappears, like the trolley buses of my childhood

Christopher Goulding

Trolleybuses – a better way of travelling

Arguably, the most environmentally friendly form of public transport in cities and towns, was the trolleybus. Silent running and with no nasty petrol or diesel fumes to pollute the atmosphere, trolleybuses were surely the kings of urban transport; faster and quieter than trams, and quieter and cleaner than motor buses. They did have some disadvantages, of course – they required traction poles to support the wires which carried the electricity that powered them. However, these traction poles usually served a dual purpose, acting also as lamp posts! Although the trolleybus was able to move short distances on its internal battery power, the need for the overhead wires meant that they were inflexible. But in spite of these drawbacks, they were the most brilliant form of urban public transport.

Tyneside boasted two trolleybus systems – South Shields and Newcastle. Newcastle owned the larger system, and one of the finest in the country. Painted bright yellow, the trolleybuses were magnificent and served not only the city centre, but travelled way out west to the old city boundary at Denton Square, beyond the eastern boundary into Wallsend, and over the northern boundary right up to Gosforth Park.

The Newcastle system began in 1935 and continued until October 1966, when the last two buses ran from Denton Square to Byker depot on service 35, and from Delaval Road to Byker depot on service 35C. Controversy reigned over which bus was actually the last one. The last one into the depot was the 23:25 from Denton Square, however, I always maintained that it should really have been the 23:29 from Delaval Road (the one which I stood and watched with a tear in my eye) but because it was a shorter journey, it arrived at Byker first!

Trolleybus 33A to Delaval Road competes for space on a crowded Northumberland Street with two motorbuses, 31 March 1956.

Trolley bus and tram in the snow on Neville Street in 1947. The trolleybus is a No. 34 from the pre-war fleet.

Tremendous service was given to the folks of Newcastle by these buses. As with most public urban transport in those halcyon days, the system was operated by the municipal authority. The operative word then, was 'service'. I lived in Benwell, where trolley buses ran every five minutes during the day and every two minutes at peak times. Even on Sundays there was a five minute frequency. On Christmas Day, a full Sunday service still operated.

Trolleybuses, in spite of being attached to the overhead wires, could hurtle along at amazing speeds. I remember once travelling the entire length of Benwell Lane/Adelaide Terrace/Elswick Road (some two miles or more) in less than four minutes. Each bus used to have its fleet number painted both inside and outside. For obvious reasons, one wag had added below the internal fleet number on one bus 'The Benwell Flyer'!

Mind you, travelling in wintertime had its unpleasant moments. Trolleybuses had no form of heating, and on many winter mornings there was ice on the inside of the windows. Wet and snowy weather could also bring problems. I remember once alighting at the stop beside the old Elswick Library. My hand was still on the metal handrail on the platform, and when my foot touched the ground a bolt of static electricity shot through me, and I ended up on my knees on the foot-path!

I always dreaded the ominous thunder from above when one or

both of the trolley booms became divorced from the overhead wire. Depending upon the agility of the conductor, re-attaching the booms to the wires could be a lengthy task. It involved taking a very long bamboo pole from its mooring (sometimes hidden behind the side panels, sometimes below the bus), hooking it onto the offending booms, and then, with great accuracy, replacing the booms onto the overhead.

As I child I was always terrified when travelling down Denton Bank, towards Denton Square. I refused to sit upstairs, as for some unknown reason, I used to think that the top deck might separate from the lower deck, and go off on its own.

With today's fears of global warming and the increase in air pollution, it would be wonderful if the great trolleybus could be revived. It was far more convenient, and, may I say, reliable, than any form of underground transport. The South Shields and Newcastle trolleybus systems were indeed, two of Tyneside's finest.

This article is dedicated to the memory of Noel Hanson; friend, colleague and local transport historian.

Douglas Bond

The A186 From Denton Road to St Nicholas Street

The West Road, towards Denton Burn, around 1930.

Newcastle's finest road runs for 5.8km roughly south-east, bisecting the West End between the Tyne and the A167 as it follows the line of the Roman Wall over a sandstone shoulder at 126m above sea level, veering off towards the Black Gate at the end. This is the proper line of the Roman Wall, not the spurious Hadrian's Wall walk by the Tyne. It is best done as a walk from west to east, as once the highest point is reached it is downhill all the way, but if you like suffering start from the Black Gate.

It begins at full gallop between Bishop's House and Hadrian's Wall, dropping down to Denton Burn. Up past the library, over the junction with Silver Lonnen and Denton Road.

Looking west on the West Road at the Fox and Hounds around 1932. By this time motorbuses had been introduced. The delivery van outside Two Ball Lonnen garage belonged to John McEwan, dairyman, of Benwell.
The map dates from 1927.

Drivers change down and walkers take deep breaths for the climb past the crematorium (a few Youngs gone that way) and the cricket ground, heaving up past school and houses, levelling out to pass the unapologetic 'Fox and Hounds' near the Two Ball Lonnen junction and on upwards to what was once the highest point in Newcastle with fine views across the Tyne Valley to Dunston Hill and Whickham.

Romans were here at Condercum Fort; cavalry patrols to the north. General Wade's men found an altar to three Celtic witches here; Antenociticus, short-lived for a god, was worshipped here just off the road. Views to the South across the Tyne must have been safer than those to the North. A long slow run now, past West Gate Community College (whither Dr. Rutherford?) (two or three Youngs more or less educated on this site).

The switchback levels out through planners' constrictions past Hindu Temple, halal shops, Jimmy's Joint, Walker's Newsagents, the Venerable Bede Church and shops galore.

Unnoticed the A186 changes name from 'West Road' to 'Westgate

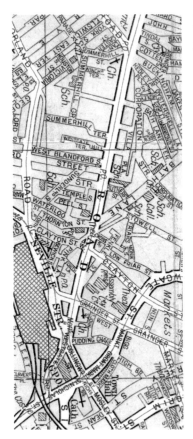

Road' where a tollhouse used to be but still keeps going, past the undertakers (a few Youngs gone there) and slopes down past the General Hospital (three Youngs born there for sure) and Police Station. The road gathers pace to pass a bowling alley. Still views to the South.

Down past Westgate Hill Primary School, and an odd little split level past the Baptist Church (a few Youngs worshipped there) and the Balmoral. Then two Courts and a Nook, out of place and out of scale. Neglected cemetery opposite, vandalised.

The road is still with the Roman Wall but the southward views are lost, replaced by those ahead to the Tyne and beyond as it cascades down Westgate Hill, stamping ground for bikers; bike shops, repair shops clinging to the hill before it skids to a stop at St James' Boulevard, dual carriageway to Gallowgate's Palace of Disappointment.

Slowing down now constricted by walls, through the line of the City walls. The switchback now a gentle slope past old Cowan and St John's Church and old Stephenson to vanish under hated Westgate House (on

The Big Lamp lights the tram wires at the junction of Elswick Road and Westgate Road around 1910. St Paul's Church is on the right.

its way out at the time of writing). Re-appears going south east(ish) past the Stamp Exchange and railway arches to reach the Black Gate and Keep and stop.

Michael Young

The long drop down Westgate Hill, 1966, and below, the last section of Westgate Road curves round to the right, past the Mining Institute towards the Castle Keep c. 1900.

Tyneside's finest places

In recent years Tyneside has frequently made national news headlines because of cutting edge architectural features such as the Sage Gateshead and Gateshead Millennium Bridge. The built heritage of the area stretches back almost two thousand years to the Roman occupation. This combination of old and new, together with natural features like the steep river gorge and the headland at the mouth of the Tyne make a visually exciting backdrop for life on Tyneside.

The Quayside

I am standing on the Quayside just to the east of the Swing Bridge, where Tyneside's history is surely made more clearly visible than at any other point. This is one of the great crossroads of Britain, where the principal north-south route up the coastal plain meets the east-west corridor formed by the valleys of the Tyne and Solway marking the island's second shortest isthmus. Newcastle owes its origins to this position at the lowest convenient bridging point on the Tyne. Here Romans built their bridge in the early second century, guarding it with

Before the Tyne Bridge. Those great industrial landmarks, the High Level Bridge and the Swing Bridge, dominate this view of the Quayside around 1890.

a fort later covered by the medieval castle. The key position favoured development of a Roman civil settlement here too.

During the middle ages a later bridge provided the same vital link for what became one of the country's principal towns. Behind me stands Newcastle's Guildhall, for many years the centre of both municipal government and the town's commerce. The building is also of historical significance for the 19th and earlier 20th centuries, for at that time it housed the Coal Exchange, the principal trading centre for coal from the Great Northern Coalfield; this provided a vital part of the energy supply which facilitated the industrialisation and urbanisation of the whole of Western Europe at a time when Europe played such a crucial role on the world stage.

Coal was also the primary resource which transformed Tyneside into one of the great industrial centres of the world, with an interlocking group of industries including coal-mining, engineering and shipbuilding that made a major contribution to the making of the modern world. Some of the elements in the long historical development are no longer visible. The appalling slums which the quayside area once saw have been swept away, as have the traces of the great fire and explosion which devastated much of riverside Newcastle and Gateshead on 6th October 1854. We can still see the High Level Bridge, which completed the main east coast railway line. The Swing Bridge enabled industrial Newcastle to expand in the western suburbs, while the Tyne Bridge signals the dominance in 20th century transport of the internal combustion engine. The King Edward VII railway bridge and the Queen Elizabeth II Metro Bridge also add to the long history of our transport links. To stand here must surely be the best vantage point from which to contemplate Tyneside's long and fascinating history.

Norman McCord

Engineering the Tyne Bridge, 1928.

John Leslie

The panoramic view from the Free Trade pub brings together many of our modern and historic landmarks from an unexpected perspective as the Tyne swings south. The silver Sage Gateshead bulges from the south bank while the spires of All Saints Church and the cathedral point skywards to the north and frame the curves of the Gateshead Millennium Bridge and the Tyne Bridge which seem to mirror each other.

Looking along the curve in the river we see a modern quayside with a rich and varied history. The area either side of the Law Courts was once a series of narrow lanes called 'chares' which from medieval times to the early 19th century provided accommodation (often cramped and dingy) for many of the poorer townsfolk. The famous 'tribe' of Keelmen who ferried coal to the mouth of the Tyne inhabited the streets around Sandgate. The heart was ripped out of the chares by a fire in 1854 and the area did not really recover until a magnificent renaissance beginning in the late 20th century gave us the landscape we see today.

Some of the landmarks in the photograph include (from the left): The Sage, designed by Norman Foster and opened in 2004; Baltic, formerly a flour mill and 1950s grain warehouse and now a centre for contemporary art designed by architects Gelder and Kitchen; the Tyne Bridge, Newcastle's iconic landmark, opened in 1928 by King George V; the Gateshead Millennium Bridge, a Sterling Prize architectural award winner, opened by Queen Elizabeth II in 2002; the Law Courts completed in 1990, housing ten Crown and three County Courts; All Saints Church, described as the finest elliptical classical church in the land, completed in 1786 to a design by David Stephenson; St Nicholas' Cathedral, founded as St Nicholas' Church in 1091 by Osamund, Bishop of Salisbury, rebuilt in 1353 and made a cathedral in 1882; the Malmaison Hotel, formerly the Co-operative Wholesale Society Warehouse and opened as a hotel following sympathetic redevelopment in 1997.

There are many spectacular views in Newcastle but this must rank as one of the finest.

❧ Jack and John Leslie

The High Level Bridge

There are probably only three candidates with a justifiable claim to be Tyneside's finest bridge, the Tyne Bridge, the Gateshead Millennium Bridge, and the High Level Bridge. The Tyne Bridge was the largest single-span bridge in Britain at the time of its formal opening in October 1928, but a larger version of this type of bridge (the Hell Gate Bridge), using a similar method of construction, had opened in New York in 1916. The Millennium Bridge is a novel moveable pedestrian bridge, and the first large Tyne bridge to be built essentially for leisure rather than commercial purposes – but in a curious way it is an anachronistic essay in bridge design, albeit a beautifully written and inspiring one, for it brings the shocking realisation that the part of the Tyne which it crosses will never again have need for full navigational clearance.

We are left with the superb High Level Bridge of 1849 by Robert Stephenson and Thomas Harrison, and its rightful claim to be regarded as Tyneside's finest bridge. In many ways it was an original construction, especially in its two-tier superstructure, but at the same time its design relied on tried and tested structural materials and engineering. Essentially, cast-iron arch ribs in parallel sets of four, their ends tied with

Detail, The High Level Bridge, 1849, J.W. Carmichael ©Newcastle University.

The new and revolutionary High Level Bridge, still unblackened, in the 1860s.

wrought-iron chains to form 'bowstring girders', rest upon five lofty ashlar-masonry piers to give six main spans. The upper rail-deck girders are supported on hollow cast-iron columns which rise from the ribs, while the lower road and footpath deck is suspended from the rail-deck girders by wrought-iron hangers which pass down inside the support columns above the ribs and matching false columns below. Cast-iron bracing frames above the side footpaths help stiffen the entire bridge structure and, incidentally, considerably add to the aesthetic pleasure of a perambulation across it. Masonry land arches at either end of the main spans climb the steep valley sides of Gateshead and Newcastle to complete the composition.

Cast iron and masonry for strength in compression, wrought iron for strength in tension, all appropriately employed with honesty and panache. Above all the High Level is fundamentally a Tyneside bridge, designed by local men, built by local masons using local stone, and local ironwork contractors. Although minor modifications have been made to the bridge since it opened nearly 160 years ago, it remains substantially unchanged from its original design, and well deserves the national recognition granted by its 'Grade I Listed' designation, a mark of its historical, engineering and cultural significance. Use it, preferably on foot, and enjoy the views of its only slightly less worthy neighbours.

Stafford M. Linsley

Steve Mayes

The photo opportunity

My interest in black and white photography only developed when I moved to Newcastle. For a while I lived on the Quayside, and the sheer volume of iconic buildings and structures that surrounded me helped foster an appreciation for architecture and photography.

The bridges are particularly inspiring, partly because they contrast so much in style. The latest addition, the Gateshead Millennium Bridge, with its graceful curves, is often the subject of my photography, especially at night when its lights are reflected in the water of the Tyne. Another favourite is the Tyne Bridge. Even after six years of living here, I still find it difficult to walk over or under it without stopping to look or photograph for a while.

Steve Mayes
www.stevemayesphotography.co.uk

Steve Mayes photographs the Tyne bridges. Previous page, Gateshead Millennium Bridge; opposite, the Tyne Bridge.

The view from the sea – Tynemouth Priory and Castle

SF

First impressions count for a lot, and for hundreds of thousands of visitors sailing into the Tyne each year there could not be a more impressive welcoming sight than the dramatic ruins of Tynemouth Priory and Castle.

They are perched on the headland, which, in the 7th century, was the site of a monastery at the mouth of the river. The monastery was attacked by Viking raiders in 800 and again 75 years later, resulting in its destruction.

The site was refounded as a Benedictine Priory in the 11th century and the 73ft-high remains of the Norman presbytery still stand. It was necessary to defend the site and by 1296 the priory was protected by 3,200ft of walls. The present gatehouse was added in the 1390s.

After the Dissolution of the monasteries the site became part of Henry VIII's national defence network and bristled with guns for centuries. During the Napoleonic Wars there were 51 guns sited at Tynemouth and in 1881 there were still 20.

By the start of the last century Tynemouth and its guns formed the controlling hub of the Tyne defence line which stretched from Blyth to Sunderland. The guns of the adjacent Spanish battery were not dismantled until the 1950s. The religious still sits alongside the military with the restored 15th century St Mary's Chapel next to the empty gun magazines.

The site is believed to have been the burial place of three kings: St Oswin the murdered King of Deira later to be absorbed into Northumbria; St Osred, King of Northumbria; and King Malcolm of Scotland after his defeat at Alnwick in 1093.

Such a prominent site had another use – as a navigational aid for shipping. An open brazier on the top of a church turret was replaced by a lighthouse tower in 1664. An oil lamp was installed in 1802.

Tony Henderson

Tynemouth Priory, lighthouse and cocoa rooms, around 1890. At this date the Priory was part of the Tyne defence line.

Historical descriptions of the topography of Newcastle frequently quote Earl Grey's description of Pilgrim Street as the 'fairest street in the towne', but we now know that the medieval alignment of the street overlies the earliest known settlement in Newcastle – a possible prehistoric farmstead. The remains of a circular building from the late Bronze Age or Iron Age, uncovered during excavations beneath the medieval buildings in the tenement behind the Market Tavern pub, suggest there may have been an ancient thoroughfare in this area, which perhaps lasted through the Roman period until the present alignment was established.

There have been no major excavations on properties in the street, so our understanding of its medieval development is largely speculative. The present name is recorded in documents of the mid-13th century, but as one of the three main streets in the early town it was probably in existence by the 1170s or slightly later – certainly early drawings of the medieval church which stood on the site of the present Georgian All Saints Church at the foot of the street show that it had Norman windows.

On the first detailed and reliable maps in the 19th century, the tenements off the northern part of the

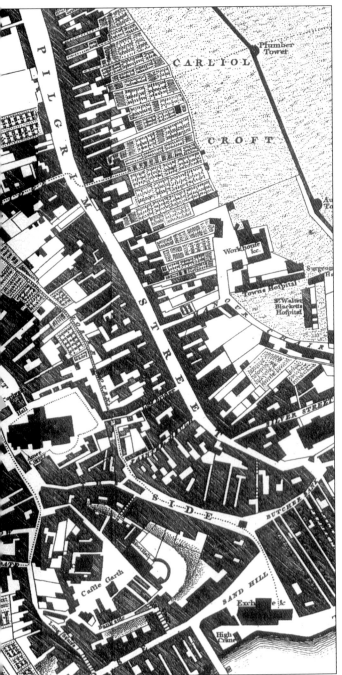

A detail from Charles Hutton's map of Newcastle, 1769.

street show a regular pattern which is typical of planned street layouts of the late 12th or early 13th centuries. It is possible that the earliest buildings were constructed at the southern end, close to the church, and development progressed north so that by the time the town wall was built in the late 13th century, it was the longest street in the town.

The street was originally called Vicus Peregrinorum. Many scholars accept this to mean the Street of Pilgrims; the Chapel of Our Lady and St Mary's Well at Jesmond or the relics of St Francis of Assisi housed

Steve Robinson

in the Grey Friars at the north end of the street are known to have been places of pilgrimage. However, at that early period the latin term *Vicus*, could indicate a district or quarter in a town rather than a street, and the translation of *Peregrinorum*, may be 'outsider or wanderer' in the sense of 'foreigner'. So the name may mean the 'foreign quarter' and have nothing to do with pilgrims at all!

The list of families living in the street in later years is impressive: the Fenwicks, Collingwoods, Ogles, Whites and Clennells among others. The grandest house, Anderson Place, was described by local historian Henry Bourne as 'very stately and magnificent, being supposed the most so of any house in the whole kingdom within a walled town', and the street itself is thought the widest ancient street in a medieval town. Of this period, Alderman Fenwick's House, restored in 1997 and one of the finest 17th century merchant's houses in the region, is a magnificent survival. Most magnificent, longest, widest and now possibly oldest, Pilgrim Street is still collecting superlatives, to which many would also add – the most interesting street in Tyneside.

David Heslop

Above, the restored cupola of Alderman Fenwick's House, Pilgrim Street, below, the house as it appeared in the 1720s.

All Saints Church

Noon, All Saints Church, around 1900.

As you drive across the Tyne Bridge from the south, you may, like me, have got into the habit of checking the time on the All Saints' Church clock on the north bank of the river. Next time you do this, traffic safety permitting, take a closer look at the church itself, its tall tapering tower with its stocky auditorium behind. You will be amazed at what you see. The church is one of the Treasures of Tyneside.

Not only is the tower a particularly elegant confection of Georgian decorated tower and stepped spire, but the oval auditorium is only one of four such in UK churches.

The original All Hallows existed on this spot before 1286. In 1785 the south aisle pillars that had supported the roof for hundreds of years began to crack marking the beginning of the end for the venerable old church; it was demolished – with the loss of at least one life – in 1786 to make way for the new. Five different architects submitted plans but, thankfully, it was the unique design of a young local architect, David Stephenson (1756-1819), that caught the eye of the local adjudicators.

By 1789, most of the church was complete and the Lord Bishop of Durham consecrated it on 17th November. Stephenson revised the design of the spire and the present one was completed in 1796, with John Burdikin, a local militiaman, standing on his head on the final stone – only 30 inches round and 194 feet above ground – to celebrate.

After 175 years of service, the church became the victim of the economic changes that led to the exodus of Quayside residents, leaving it high and dry. It was deconsecrated in 1961 and purchased by the City Council in 1970. They cleaned off its Victorian grime and kept it wind and water tight.

Town Teacher Limited leased the church in 1983 for use as an urban studies centre and cultural auditorium. I was happy to sign the lease as Founder/Chair of Town Teacher because bringing into use such a unique historic building directly benefited my daily work as a Conservation Officer with Tyne and Wear County Council.

In the subsequent restoration, generously funded by the City Council, an additional fire exit had to be installed. In order to stay in character with this Grade I building, the modern exit doors were hidden from inside the church by a sliding panel while the outside door is in fact a section of the original stone church wall which magically moves outwards on rails! This ingenious solution is consistent with the two early hidden doors already inside the church.

So, All Saints Church is something special on Tyneside. But don't just take my word for it; here is what others have said: 'This structure

is decidedly the most splendid architectural ornament, which modern times have produced in this town' – Thomas Sopwith, *History of All Saints Church*, 1826; one of Newcastle's 'most treasured possessions' – Sir John Betjeman, late Poet Laureate; 'Original in its plan and most effective in its exterior' – Nicholas Pevsner, *Buildings of Northumberland*, 1957 and 1992.

David Lovie

A word or a phrase can sometimes set off a chain reaction of thought. 'Would you like to contribute to a book to be called 'Tyneside's Finest'?' I was asked. If 'New York's Finest' was its police force, then was 'Tyneside's Finest' the former Newcastle City Police that I joined in 1954? But then I thought better of travelling down that particular train of thought; my good friends from the other old and smaller forces on each side of the Tyne would have given me a very hard time.

However, I put forward the former headquarters of that force, the police, fire and courts complex at Pilgrim Street and Market Street as the finest of its kind on Tyneside and a handsome landmark in the heart of the city of Newcastle upon Tyne.

The building was designed by Cacket, Burns Dick and McKellar of Newcastle to replace the ornate courts and police headquarters of 1874 at the corner of Pilgrim Street and Worswick Street. The official opening of the whole complex was on Friday 16 June 1933 with Sir Russell

The brand new police headquarters nears completion, surrounded by trolleybus wires.

Anna Flowers

Anna Flowers

Scott, Permanent Secretary of State at the Home Office doing the honours. The courts and police station had actually been in use since 1931 to enable the old building to be demolished to make way for the new fire station. There are sound security reasons for housing courts and police in connecting buildings. Linking police to fire stations had its roots in the joint history of police and fire services and is not necessary today.

The clean lines of the design and finishing in Portland limestone combined to create a distinguished building of substance and quiet dignity well suited to its purpose. Novocastrians can take a pride in the building which is a perfect foil for Carliol House on the opposite corner. The architects designed colonnades along the upper floors to face Market Street and Pilgrim Street. At each end of the two rows of columns are carvings of griffins, four in all. The author of the programme for the official opening said this about the griffins: 'The mythical animal with the body of a lion, conventional wings and the head of an eagle, suggests the attributes of Power, Watchfulness and Swiftness to act, qualities equally appropriate to the operation of the Law as to the duties of the Fire Brigade.'

I first entered the police headquarters through the revolving door to be interviewed by the Chief Constable early in 1954. His police clerk took me to one side and said in a whisper 'If the Chief asks you if you drink, say yes in moderation.' The Chief did ask and I duly replied as advised, but that was the truth you see! Years later, in the 1980s, major improvements to the police premises were necessary. I had achieved senior rank by then and I vividly recall a conversation outside the main entrance with Superintendent Tom Telfer, who was in charge there, and the engineer supervising the renovations. The once fine bronze lamps on each side of the door were tatty, neglected and minus globes. At my request the lamps were taken down, restored and fitted with blue globes. The restored lamps enhanced that part of the building and to this day, in retirement, I take some pride in seeing the gentle glow of the lights at night.

Barry Redfern

Grey Street – architectural masterpiece

Until the 1780s, the line now occupied by Grey Street and Dean Street was the steep-sided valley of one of Newcastle's old rivers, the Lort Burn. The southern portion of the valley was then culverted and developed to form Dean Street. Further north, the valley was developed in early Victorian years into Grey Street, a central feature of the new town centre created by Richard Grainger, with the co-operation of the town council and a group of distinguished local architects. Grainger also needed entrepreneurial skill to ensure success – he persuaded the Bank of England to take Grey Street premises before the Bank appreciated that the building straddled a parochial boundary, involving two sets of rates, but also conventional responsibility for supporting philanthropic activities in two separate parishes.

The architecture of Grey Street exploited a range of symmetrical and stylish classical frontages, a form which may have seemed a little old-fashioned by then but which has ensured that the street has received high praise ever since its completion. In a celebrated (and much stage-managed) visit to Newcastle in 1862, Gladstone praised the street as one of the finest in England, perhaps in Europe (though his credibility may be diminished by his declaration on the same occasion that in America the Confederates seemed to be making a nation!). A century later, Sir John Betjeman recollected: 'I shall never forget seeing it to perfection, traffic-less on a misty Sunday morning. Not even Regent Street, even old Regent Street in London, can compare with that descending subtle curve.'

Grey Street was designed to become part of the commercial heart of the regional capital, with banks, insurance companies and similar enterprises prominent among its occupiers. Industrial and mining enterprises often placed commercial headquarters there. Newcastle's eminence owed much to its provision of facilities needed to service the region during the Victorian boom period – commerce, banking, insurance, recreation, accommodation – activities which became increasingly complex, as one simple example illustrates. When Grey Street was built, the insurance sector was already important, but its services were limited in scope and affected only a small minority. By inter-war years one office in Grey Street was offering insurance for; Fire, life, marine, annuities, domestic servants, burglary, motor cars, personal accidents, fidelity guarantees, workmen's compensation, boiler, engineering, plate

One of the treasures of the Local Studies collection is this very early photograph of Grey Street's elegant curve, less than 30 years after its completion. Even then, grime had covered the sandstone.

glass and loss of profits.

Some of us can remember Grey Street when generations of grime had given the street a dark, dirty facade (and even those remarkable years in which, as piecemeal cleaning progressed, the street had a piebald aspect!). In a period of cleaner air, it has recovered its distinguished appearance, and Grey Street is now one of the showpieces of the region and an acknowledged architectural masterpiece.

᪐ *Norman McCord*

Grainger Street – a childhood memory

I've always loved Newcastle, but when I was a child, around 75 years ago, the most magical street of all was Grainger Street.

St John's Church on the corner always seemed quiet, peaceful and remote, even though it stood in one of the busiest parts of town. On a low stool against the churchyard wall, her rusty skirts around her feet, sat the match lady. She was there every day, summer and winter, morning till night. This outdoor life had taken its toll on her appearance. Her face was red, her nose was raw, her hair tangled down her face. In summer she wore a battered straw hat which she exchanged in winter for faded black felt.

Across the lane was the fairytale castle that was the gas company showroom and offices. With its delicate spires, marble floors and staircase it really was an enchanting place. It later became Wengers department store. On the opposite side of the road was Ye Olde Dickens bakery and tea room. The waitresses there wore black dresses with white caps and aprons.

Less salubrious was the Grainger Cinema, which was dark, shabby and (literally) ratty. One lady we knew actually saw a rat munching a sandwich which had been dropped underneath one of the seats. I went there only once, to catch a film I'd missed everywhere else. I was so nervous about the possibility of vermin scurrying round in the dark that I hardly dared put my feet on the floor.

Fairytale swags on the Gas Company in 1935, festooned for the Coronation.

A bustling Grainger Street, 1924, the Grainger Market on the left.

Then there was the Grainger Market which was always exciting. There was a wonderful toy stall at the Nun Street end. It was banked up high with toys and there was a small platform at the front so that little people like me could see all the wares. I loved the smell of the plant and flower stalls.

The market stayed open late, and in the evenings there was a very different atmosphere. The relative quiet and the lofty roof made it all seem quite romantic. My most special memory is of the Christmas when I was five and my father took me to the Grainger Market one evening to buy a tree. It was wonderful. The market was almost deserted, the lights were dim and the ice cream stalls were shuttered. There was hardly anyone about. The Christmas tree seller stood in a corner. He didn't have a stall and his trees were leaning against the wall. He patiently showed us lots of trees until we found one that was just right. He tied it up with string so we could carry it home.

It was now dusk. The shops and lamp posts were lit up and the traffic hushed. We passed the hot chestnut man who stood at the top of Grainger Street day and night. His machine gave off a wonderful warm red glow. We caught the tramcar. It was quiet at that time of night so there was plenty of room for us and our tree. Travelling home we looked through the tram windows at the flower ladies, still at their posts along Grainger Street.

Agnes Chilton

I love wandering around markets. I attribute this fondness for them to my childhood visits to Newcastle's Grainger Market. Designed by John Dobson and built by Richard Grainger as part of their city improvement plan in the early part of the 19th century, this was Newcastle's original shopping mall. When it opened in 1835 it was the world's largest indoor market.

I enjoy the fact that the country's oldest Marks and Spencer's stall still trades there and that I can buy books, bird seed, boots or brisket beneath its wide arching roof.

We lived in Whitley Bay, but my mother was a Novocastrian. Born and brought up on Percy Street, Mam missed the city and would devise all sorts of excuses 't'gan t'the toon'. Usually this meant that we'd end up visiting the Grainger Market and Aunty Sally's flower stall.

Our first stop was always the Weigh House, 'accurate to the last ounce,' Mam would declare. There was always a queue; few people owned bathroom scales. Come to think of it, few had bathrooms.

Aunty Sally was the 'glamour puss' and career woman of the family. Independent and outspoken, I was in awe of her. Smartly turned-out, with permed hair and bright red lipstick, she wore a green apron

SF

over a cotton overall. On her hands there were fingerless gloves, the first I'd ever seen. Sally was a divorcee; in the puritanical late 40's this gave her a delicious air of wicked sophistication in my eyes.

Her shop was in what was then the Green Market (now the Arcade) and light flooded down into this area from vaulted glass roof high above. In springtime the delicate, pollen-sweet perfume of daffodils insinuated itself into the air around. In summer, the tall green buckets for flowers and foliage held masses of bright blooms and the scent of carnations and roses wafted warmly up the surrounding aisles Autumn/winter brought the spicy aroma of chrysanthemums and pine needles mixed with the wet wool/old dog smell of people's clothing and the damp, muddy concrete of the floor. Underlying the whole was the leafy-

The Grainger Market, 1949.

green fragrance of the Green Market: the earthiness of soil-streaked potatoes, cabbages, carrots and parsnips piled artistically on the adjoining fruit and vegetable stalls, with an occasional and insidious whiff of meat from the butchers' stalls in the Grainger Market.

Whilst Mollie and Sally boasted and bickered together – and believe me, at times the sibling rivalry between the two was almost tangible – stallholders around about them would yell to passers-by, 'Hoo, hinny, carrots and turnips for yer stew pot. Get your bargains here!'

When I left school I worked in Newcastle and would visit Sally sometimes during lunchtime wanderings around the Grainger Market. She provided all the flowers for my wedding, as she did for my sisters.

We were about to move south when I last met her, by chance, in a Northumbrian country pub. In her sixties, still smartly-dressed, she was with a handsome man, rather younger than herself. I greeted her warmly as 'Aunty Sally' but she glowered at me. When her friend went to the bar for drinks, she whispered furiously, 'Call me Sally, and drop all that aunty stuff. I divent want my friend to think I'm Methusalah's daughter, y'knaa.'

I still love the Grainger Market and I'm glad it is still around as a part of Newcastle's historical past and mine.

Maureen Brook

The beautiful Central Arcade fronts on to three streets, Grainger Street, Grey Street and Market Street. It is a listed building, constructed between 1834 and 1838 as the 'Central Exchange and News Room', by Richard Grainger to a design by John Wardle. Grainger originally planned it as a corn exchange. The building was officially opened to great acclaim on 17 June 1839.

The 'Exchange' was a commercial trading centre and a newspaper reading facility. In its heyday it boasted up to 1,500 subscribers who each paid one guinea for the privilege of membership. In 1867 it was almost destroyed by fire along with number of other businesses housed in the building. Extensive restoration was required but, lacking support, the Exchange and News Room was closed in 1869. The following year the building was re-launched as an Art Gallery (still incorporating a news room). The 400 works of art housed in the Gallery were described as the best ever seen in Newcastle.

The Central Arcade elegantly dominates the Grey's Monument area around 1900.

The art gallery and news room, 1880.

In 1891 the interior was remodelled to provide further public rooms with the aim of creating a centre for social and cultural activities. The refurbished Exchange offered both Ladies' and Gentlemen's reading rooms on the first floor, a smoke and chess room, billiard room, art gallery, meeting room, refreshments areas and toilets. There were also photography and art clubs. In 1893 a concert hall opened within the art gallery; this was described as being of beautiful design with perfect acoustics, and had a capacity for 1,000 people. Subscriptions for this amazing facility were £1 11s 6d for gentlemen and £1 1s for ladies. Members' sons and gentlemen living more than seven miles away were charged the same as ladies. Daughters (unmarried) were charged 15 shillings.

A second fire in 1901 once again destroyed the interior of the building and from 1904 the Laing Art Gallery provided the city with a purpose-built home for fine art.

The Central Arcade, as we now know it, opened again in 1906 after extensive refurbishment. This regal building is in the Corinthian style, uniform in design on all three sides. It has three high ribbed domes topped by the Prince of Wales feathers and the architecture and aesthetic finish inside the arcade, with its glistening Burmantofts faience, is a marvel for residents and visitors alike.

Jack and John Leslie

St Nicholas' Cathedral tower

Like any landmark that is seen by many people every day, the spire of St Nicholas' cathedral can be taken for granted. It suffers from standing in a rather busy skyline where it is crowded out by modern buildings of considerably less character. But closer study of the graceful vaulting that effortlessly supports the great weight of the lantern chamber will reveal that the structure is an almost perfect and faultless solution to the problems created by that form of tower.

The bell tower is dated, on both architectural and documentary evidence, to the period around 1470. The inscription 'Ornate pro anima Roberti de Rodes' which is carved on the inner face of the octagonal gap at the crown of the vault – to let the sound of the bells resonate around the church and facilitate the lifting of the bells into the ringing chamber – describes the spire as 'decorated for the soul of Robert Rhodes' a prominent Newcastle merchant and benefactor to several churches, who died in 1474.

The specific form of tower is known as a 'Scottish Crown' as it is a design more common north of the border. The only other example in England is St Dunstan-in-the-East, London. The best known Scottish example is St Giles, Edinburgh, in the paved square off the Royal Mile; it is squat and heavy compared to Newcastle's soaring pinnacles.

The tower has always been maintained by the Corporation of Newcastle rather than the cathedral chapter, and according to popular legend this is because the town wanted to keep a light in the tower to guide travellers across the town moor. There is a document of a payment by the Mayor of Newcastle in 1566 for 'four pounds of wax made in the candle for the lantern of St Nicholas' Church'.

SF

Significantly, this arrangement also gave the town control of the bells and bell-ringing, and enabled civic occasions to be celebrated as well as religious festivals and services. The city still pays the bell-ringers to play three times a year – for Commonwealth Day, the Queen's Birthday and Lord Mayor's Day. Sadly, we have stopped ringing on August 4th each year – the Queen Mother's birthday.

Notable architects employed by the city to undertake repairs on the lantern and its supporting buttresses include John Green and John Dobson in the 1830s, Sir George Gilbert Scott in 1868, who underset the tower with concrete foundations (the medieval walls were set on the ground) and Richard John Leeson, who in 1895 replaced the sections of

The graceful lantern tower of St Nicholas, captured in 1932.

the pinnacles which were starting to crumble. The one architect whose name we don't know is the original designer of the structure but his work lives on to be admired by all who take the trouble to look, 600 years after the spire was built.

David Heslop

One of Newcastle's less familiar institutions is, perhaps, the library of the Literary and Philosophical Society, the Lit & Phil as it is more affectionately known. Completed in 1825, the building has continued virtually in its original form ever since.

The Lit & Phil began as a learned body based on Birmingham's 'Lunar Society'. Principally the brain-child of the Reverend William Turner, it was founded in 1793 although it was not until 1822 that plans to build new premises came to fruition. In September of that year there was a grand ceremonial stone-laying attended by the Duke of Sussex. The highlight of the day, however, was the dinner in the Assembly Rooms which was followed by a marathon session of 53 speeches and 35 toasts!

This event was (thankfully) not characteristic of the society's future activities and during the 19th century it was the centre for learning in Newcastle. In the years before the establishment of professional bodies and universities, the town's scientists, engineers, industrialists and others met there to discuss a great variety of subjects. It was at the Lit & Phil (but not in the present building) that George Stephenson showed his newly-invented miners' lamp in 1817; William George Armstrong first spoke on electricity in 1844; and Joseph Wilson Swan demonstrated the first incandescent electric light in 1880. The society's past presidents include three of the nation's greatest engineers: Robert Stephenson, Lord W.G. Armstrong and Sir Charles Parsons. Not all of the society's events, however, have been so happy: in October 1844 its water closet was the scene of a suicide (the victim, his throat cut with a penknife, was not discovered until a week had elapsed) and in 1893, immediately after its centenary celebrations and within hours of the end of a lecture by Lord Armstrong, again on electricity, the building was almost completely destroyed by fire.

The society was the inspiration for the formation of other institutions in Newcastle – the Natural History Society and the North of England Institute of Mining and Mechanical Engineers. Today its members are still able to enjoy its ambience, its architecture and its splendid collection of books, both old and new.

The Lit and Phil in 1825.

❧ *Robert W. Rennison*

Newcastle Central Station in the 1950s.

For 150 years the Central Station has been the gateway to Newcastle. Passengers from the south would cross Stephenson's impressive High Level Bridge with views over the coaly Tyne, then sweep past the remains of the ancient Castle Keep, over the diamond crossing, the world's most complicated rail crossing, to arrive at the magnificent edifice which is Central Station. Elsewhere in this book, you will find a description of John Dobson's architecture, but I'd like to tell you a tale of when I was briefly employed in the Enquiry Office during the late 1950's.

I began by sitting with Olive, a neat and dainty young woman who knew how to get anyone to anywhere. Eventually she judged me ready to 'fly solo', so the next Monday morning I climbed apprehensively onto my stool to face the public. At my elbow was *Bradshaw's Guide* – the encyclopaedia of railway timetables – and a notebook and pencil. At 8.45am. the first customer, a rather harried-looking young man in jeans and jacket arrived. The five other clerks put their heads down. I sat up, bright-eyed and smiling. He had no choice, it had to be me! 'Umm, I want to send an elephant to London.' An elephant? To London? I swallowed hard. Something more along the lines of, 'I want to go to Manchester on Wednesday and have to be there at 9.30,' was what I'd anticipated. Flustered, I glanced along the counter at my colleagues hoping that someone had overheard and would rescue me. Instead, every head was down. Such utter indifference bordered on the suspicious and I began to suspect a prank. Young and inexperienced I might be, but green I was not. They'd not catch me out with somebody's boyfriend making artless enquiries about elephants. I turned my attention back to the young man and smiled sweetly. 'Would that be an African elephant or an Indian elephant?' I asked, raising my voice to indicate that I was playing along with the joke. He looked puzzled, which confirmed my suspicion he was a plant! 'Indian,' he replied slowly.

'A male or female elephant, sir?'

'Why do you want to know that?' he frowned.

'I was thinking of the weight, sir.' I took a surreptitious glance along the counter and smugly noted my colleagues were beginning to sit up. 'And the colour, sir?'

At this, the man began to look cross, 'It's an elephant. It's grey. What colour do you expect it to be, man, pink?'

I smiled again, 'Nothing would surprise me, Sir. Not even pink elephants.'

At this point I was saved from making a complete idiot of myself when Olive's voice interrupted quietly. 'I think, Sir, we need to refer you to our freight department who have special facilities for transporting animals.' She wrote down an address and telephone number for him. As the man turned away, she asked, 'May I enquire, sir, why you are sending an elephant to London?'

'Of course,' he said, turning back to us, 'It's been in the pantomime at the Theatre Royal but it's needed at Covent Garden for an opera. It's an experienced performer, you know.'

In another two weeks I realised the job really wasn't for me and I left. There was, however, an unexpected postscript. Twice a week I'd had to collect the pennies from the doorlocks in the ladies' toilets, helped by Nora, the attendant, but from that time onwards, I never needed another penny at Central Station.

⁂ Maureen Brook

If you read older books about architecture you get the impression that any sort of regional variation in the style of building disappeared at about the time the railways arrived. Improved transport, they imply, carried ideas as well as goods and people and as a result everywhere began to look like everywhere else. Not true. Lots of parts of the country continued to follow unique patterns and to invent local solutions to local problems well into the 20th century.

Or to put it another way, the Tyneside Flat.

Tyneside Flats are – I'm sure you know this but it has to be said – Tyneside Flats are two-storey terraced flats. They look superficially like

Working-class Tyneside flats. A rainy day on Shields Road, 20 June, 1901.

And the posher variety with bay windows – Thornleigh Road, Jesmond, 1910.

ordinary streets of terraced houses but each property has two doors side by side – one to the downstairs flat and one to the upstairs. At the back, by a bit of cunning wheezery, both flats have their own private bit of back yard. Flats with two exterior doors and a bit of privacy, that is cunning isn't it? They can be quite big too. I have friends with Tyneside flats in Jesmond which are distinctly middle-class in scale while others are smaller and more intimate (it's the flats I'm talking about, not my friends).

Tyneside Flats seem to have been invented sometime after 1850 and they went on being built well into the 20th century. They were fantastically popular. Almost 50% of the population of Tyneside lived in flats in the early 20th century. That compares to less than 4% in other urban areas of the country. Nobody knows who invented them, or why this particular form came to be common here but whoever the designer was he, or indeed she, did a clever thing because Tyneside flats turned out to be a brilliant way to house far more people in relative luxury on a smaller area of land than conventional houses could possibly have done.

The final thing I like about them is that they're unique to Tyneside. Actually that's a lie, they aren't unique to Tyneside. There are similar (but fancier) terraced flats in south London and the books say there are some in Carlisle though, as a Carlisle lad, I can't think where they are. But on Tyneside they are everywhere. They are one of the things that define us.

᪥ *John Grundy*

Lemington Glass Cone – the North East's own pyramid

There was once a time when, with a little experience, the purpose of many an industrial building could be determined by its very structure, or the nature of an industry by a particular grouping of identifiable buildings. Brickworks, potteries, maltings, kipper curing sheds, windmills, electric power stations, traditional rope walks and collieries were obvious examples. Other industrial buildings, however, often defied such simple recognition. For example, one of Tyneside's finest industrial buildings, the former Wills cigarette factory on the Coast Road, was so unlike a traditional factory building that it was recently converted into very desirable apartments.

For an industrial building to merit the attribution of 'Tyneside's Finest', it must surely tell us directly of its past or present function. In other words it must characterise or define the industry of which it is, or was, a part. A story from Australia, which may or may not be apocryphal, might help us here. It is said that when Captain Cook spotted a

Lemington Glass Cone towers above another well-known Tyneside institution, the allotment, in 1976.

range of hills some 50 miles north of Brisbane, all shaped like large cones, he named them the Glasshouse Mountains because of his familiarity with the immediately recognisable glassworks' cones along parts of the North East coast and the rivers Tyne and Wear. Tyneside's finest industrial building has to be the 'Glass Cone' at Lemington on Tyne.

Lemington glassworks was launched in 1787 under a partnership originally known as 'The Northumberland Glass Company'. The location was ideal for local coal supplies, but rather less so for the necessary imports of suitable clays for the melting pots and the sand and alkali which are melted together to form glass. Initially flat glass was the main product and over the next few years four large glass cones were erected, the largest of which remains on site, standing some 120 feet high and reputed to have used 1.75 million bricks when it was built in 1797.

Such cones were the standard form of glasshouse in the North East from about the middle of the 19th century. Their main function was to house a much smaller centrally-located domed circular or rectangular furnace which held between eight and ten melting pots. Each pot provided the melt for a team of three co-workers. The furnace heating was provided by under-floor coal fires, and the furnace dome provided reverberatory heating action. The enveloping cone assisted the furnace draught while simultaneously keeping the workers cool, but also sheltered the melting furnace, materials, products and workers from the elements, and housed annealing furnaces, workbenches, tools, etc. The glass cone, in short, enclosed the glass factory. Glassmaking stopped at Lemington around 1997, and almost all the factory buildings were demolished to make way for motor car and heating stove showrooms.

The large cone was, however, retained. As one of only four such cones to survive in Britain, this is one of the most important industrial monuments in the country, let alone in the North East, and an outstanding example of functional industrial architecture. The Lemington glass cone is the nearest the North East has to an Egyptian Pyramid, and like those ancient structures it must be seen from inside to be fully appreciated.

Stafford M. Linsley

All big cities have their open spaces, mostly relics of Victorian or Edwardian civic pride. These parks, if they haven't received a lottery-funded makeover, are often sad and sometimes scary. Newcastle's unique Town Moor is not loved in the sense that it has had millions spent on it. Yet it is loved by many who find its open acres as fresh and invigorating as a sea dip.

As a country boy with an aversion to cities, this accident of urban town planning – or rather, perhaps, this escapee from urban town planning – was part of what made Newcastle alluring when I moved here. Skylarks were part of the soundtrack of my childhood in rural Dorset; the same soaring birdsong you will hear over this tufted moorland in the heart of a city.

Many are the developers who must have eyed it covetously. I know of one urban regenerator who regarded it as a wasted resource. But quirks of history and possibly of geology (there are lots of little bogs underfoot) mean the cows, the skylarks, the joggers, the dog walkers,

The Town Moor hoppings, 1957.

Anthony Flowers

the idle strollers, the refugees from urban stress and those merely taking a short cut through some unhindered views have it all to themselves.

Historians tell us the Town Moor dates from at least 1357 when Edward III granted a charter to Newcastle confirming possession of 89 acres of common land. The total moorland area now amounts to about 1,000 acres with the central Town Moor, flanked by Grandstand Road, Claremont Road and the Great North Road, accounting for 349.

It is controlled jointly by Newcastle City Council, who own the land, and the rather mysterious Freemen of the City who have grazing rights. Sometimes I imagine I hear, carried on the wind, the eerily time-lapsed cheers of race goers. Horses competed here in the 18th and 19th centuries until the race meetings were moved to Gosforth Park. A pleasure denied to those cheering hordes was the view of the distant Cheviots from the top of the twin mounds created when the Central Motorway was dug out.

Every year the sound of revels returns. The Hoppings, a huge fun-fair, appears for a week and then, like a summer mirage, disappears, giving way once again to a silence broken only by the wind, the skylarks and – if you choose to hear it – the hum of distant traffic.

❧ *David Whetstone*

They say we're related we Skyetenders, either by marriage or drink. The name comes from 'skuet,' an old word meaning to cure fish. You're a Skyetender then if, like me, you were born on the headland of the Lawe in South Shields – the 'sheels' itself another ancient word, for fishing huts.

This was where the Romans built Arbeia, their fort and supply base for Hadrian's Wall.

It must have conditioned them for manning their most northerly border in England. In winter, gales, salt-laden and abrading, drive straight in off the North Sea, pinching faces and shrivelling the paint-work of our 19th century houses – for I still live there.

Each terrace climbs a little higher than the last one up the hill, virtually every other home, once upon the time, the address of a Tyne pilot, master mariner, sea-going engineer, lifeboatman or crew member of a tug or foyboat.

The Lawe is an island on some old maps, bounded by the sea, the

South Tyneside MBC

Beyond the ships is the Lawe Top, with its Victorian terraces, around 1870.

Tyne and a tributary of the river to the south that once ran inland and out again into the German Ocean, as it used to be called, among rocks, and sand and ragged ballast hills.

These hills are now the town's Marine Parks, though if you scratch around on the slopes of the northern-most park, you can still find gnarled lumps of glassworks waste, reddened and black, as if they still held the somnolent heat of the great glass furnaces.

We called these banks 'the middens' when we played on them as children, not knowing that this word, too, reached back in time to the wholesale depositing of both glass and chemical works filth on the shoreline, as well as ships' ballast.

Words. They set the place apart just as much as it was once cut-off geographically. You can hear it in the speech: 'Laa' for 'Lawe' and 'tow', to rhyme with 'cow'.

You're a Skyetender, it's said, if you've still got a ring round your backside (from the bucket, you see, outside netties in bitter weather being as distant and to be avoided as Siberia, from which the wind – it's true, look at an Atlas – blows in along the same parallel).

Fish curing has long since vanished from the riverside below the Lawe. But on certain days in mid-winter, when a familiar reek drifts over from the direction of North Shields and the wind-blown brine dries salty on your lips, coming up home to the Skyetend still feels like leaving the 21st century behind.

Janis Blower

Tyneside's finest people

It's probably fair to say that Tyneside's finest asset is its people. Courageous, determined, inventive, athletic – the area is full of heroes. Some are household names, others known only to those closest to them. If we were to include all of Tyneside's finest people this book would be an encyclopaedia; instead we asked contributors to celebrate just a few of the people who have helped to make Tyneside great.

War heroes

Tommy Brown, GM (1927-1945)

Tynesider Tommy Brown is the youngest person to be awarded the George Medal. He won the award at the age of 16 for an act of bravery performed in connection with the capture of German naval codebooks during the Second World War.

The breaking of German codes made a major contribution to Allied victory. Some military historians believe it shortened the war by as much as two years. The centre of code breaking operations was located at Bletchley Park in Buckinghamshire, where a team of boffins successfully cracked Germany's military codes. German naval codes, however, proved difficult to break until the capture of Kriegsmarine codebooks.

On 30 October 1942 the destroyer HMS *Petard* tracked a U-boat in the Eastern Mediterranean. At 2200 hours the German submarine U-559 surfaced and her crew began to abandon ship. First Lieutenant F.A.B Fasson and two other crew men from the *Petard*, Colin Grazier and Kenneth Lacroix, followed by Tommy Brown a young canteen assistant, boarded the scuttled submarine with the aim of securing its codebooks before it sank.

Fasson and Grazier went below and smashed open the cabinets containing the books, while Lacroix and Brown made three trips carrying the books up the ladder to the deck of the submarine. Fasson and Grazier left it too late to escape and were drowned but Lacroix and Brown were able to swim to safety. The captured codebooks proved invaluable to the Bletchley cryptographers and young Tommy Brown, was awarded the George Medal. For security reasons the award was not given much publicity at the time.

Thomas William Brown was born in North Shields in 1927 and he attended the western Board School. When he left school he wanted to join the Royal Navy but was too young. However, at the age of 16 he was taken on as a canteen assistant by the NAAFI and posted to HMS *Petard*. He was, therefore, a non-combatant member of the crew when he helped to rescue the codebooks from the sinking U-boat. He did not live long enough to enjoy any kind of fame: on 13 November 1945, when on leave, he died of asphyxia in a fire at his home in North Shields while trying to rescue his four year old sister from an upstairs bedroom. There is a stained glass window dedicated to his memory at the Saville Exchange building in North Shields.

Archie Potts

Admiral Collingwood – Northumberland's heart of oak

Tyneside's greatest hero was also perhaps its most reluctant warrior. Cuthbert Collingwood ought to have followed his father into the family business, as a trader on Newcastle's bustling Side – a narrow winding street that led down to the Quayside – but the business went bust. Without money, both the law and the army were impossible careers. So at the age of 13, in 1761, the boy went to sea as a captain's servant, to be trained as a naval officer.

It was a long, hard apprenticeship. Collingwood served in frigates as a midshipman and master's mate for 14 years before the chance of action finally led to his promotion to lieutenant. By then he was a highly experienced and able sailor. After being given charge of the

boats ferrying men and ammunition to Charlestown in June 1775 at the Battle of Bunker's Hill, his coolness and bravery under fire, which would later be legendary, were proven.

The following years were of mixed fortune. He served under a rotten, tyrannical commander in the West Indies before Nelson, whom he had first met in 1773, brought him to the attention of Sir Peter Parker. Parker recognised his talents and gave him his crucial promotion to Post Captain. Collingwood and Nelson would remain friends until Nelson's death.

Collingwood gazes out to sea from his memorial at North Shields. The gun is from Royal Sovereign, his ship at Trafalgar.

It was the war against France, which began in 1793, that propelled both Nelson and Collingwood onto a stage where their different but complementary talents could be given full rein. Nelson was impetuous, vain, charismatic, a brilliant battle commander. Collingwood, though in private – as his letters show – a witty, warm and charming man of great erudition, was in public reserved. His genius as a sea commander was in his management of men, his extraordinary insouciance and his diplomatic skills. In the months before Trafalgar he saw off the entire French fleet with a squadron of just three ships – without firing a shot.

At Trafalgar he led the lee line of battleships; was the first to fire and the first to be fired on. He was seen calmly munching an apple on his quarterdeck as, one by one, his officers were cut down around him. And when, at about four in the afternoon, he was informed of the death of the Commander-in-Chief he wept for the loss of a friend, as the rest of the fleet wept for the loss of their hero. His achievement in ensuring that not a single British ship was lost during the ensuing terrible storm was, according to Earl St Vincent, 'above all praise'.

After fighting in three of the great actions of the war – including the Battle of Cape St Vincent where he came to Nelson's rescue with an awesome display of naval gunnery – he himself became Commander-in-Chief of the Mediterranean, and it was as virtual viceroy that he proved himself indispensable to the British government. In a staggering seven-year tour of duty he dealt with deys, beys, pashas, emperors and sultans, ensuring a Mediterranean coalition against Napoleon that led directly to the Peninsula War and Wellington's final victory. That Trafalgar is remembered as the last great naval action of the age of sail is substantially due to Collingwood. Tragically, during that period between 1803 and his death in 1810, he never saw England, his beloved wife or two daughters. He died at sea having, like Nelson, given his life to his country.

What surprises us, in looking back at his life 200 years on, is his humanity, his wit, and his modernity of outlook. But for his more celebrated friend and comrade he might well be our national naval hero. In later years W.M. Thackeray said he thought that since heaven made gentlemen, there was no record of a better one than Collingwood. It is perhaps a fitting epitaph for a man who, though he spent 44 years at sea as a warrior, wished for the most part to be at home with his family in Morpeth, tending his roses and digging over his long-neglected cabbage patch.

Max Adams

John Simpson Kirkpatrick – the man with the donkey

As a youngster John Simpson Kirkpatrick worked during the summers giving donkey rides to children at a fun fair in his home town of South Shields. After finishing work at 9pm, he would ride a donkey home and so developed his affinity with the animals.

Some years later, John become known as 'The Man with the Donkey' because of his actions during the murderous and ill-fated Gallipoli campaign in Turkey during the First World War. Over 24 days he rescued scores of wounded men under constant enemy fire.

John was born in 1892 to merchant seaman Robert and his wife Sarah. He left South Shields at the age of 17 on the SS *Heighington* and later joined the crew of the *Yedda* as stoker, sailing for Newcastle in Australia. There he left the ship and worked his way around the country, cattle droving, cane cutting, coal mining, trying his luck on the gold fields and on coastal vessels. He always sent generous portions of his pay home to South Shields.

The statue at South Shields. Eyewitness accounts record the donkey's name as Murphy, Duffy, or Elizabeth, among others. There may have been more than one donkey.

The Man with the Donkey, Melbourne.

John enlisted three weeks after the outbreak of the First World War and was assigned to the Field Ambulance section of the Australian army. He was part of the force which landed at Gallipoli in April 1915 and suffered appalling casualties as the Australians were pinned down by Turkish troops occupying the high ground.

Acquiring several donkeys, John worked alone, rescuing and carrying wounded men from the head of a valley down what was known as Shrapnel Gulley to the beach. As first he seemed to have a charmed life but on May 10 he was killed by a burst of machine gun fire.

Padre George Green, who officiated at John's burial service, said: 'I often remember the scene I saw frequently in Shrapnel Gully of that cheerful soul calmly walking down the gully with a Red Cross armlet tied around the donkey's head. That gully was under direct fire from the enemy almost all the time.'

The official Australian war historian C.E.W. Bean wrote: 'He escaped death so many times that he was completely fatalistic. He saved many lives at the cost of his own.'

Gallipoli officer Colonel John Monash said: 'He was worth a hundred men to me.'

John is now commemorated by statues in South Shields; Melbourne, Australia; on a frieze at Gallipoli; and in paintings held in Canberra and Auckland, New Zealand. He has also been depicted on three Australian postage stamps.

Tony Henderson

Private Edward Lawson VC

Alan Morgan

PRIVATE
EDWARD LAWSON
1st BATTALION
THE GORDON HIGHLANDERS
AWARDED THE VICTORIA CROSS
ON THE NORTH WEST FRONTIER
20th OCTOBER 1897
AND WHO DIED 2nd JULY 1955
AGED 82 YEARS.

ALSO HIS SON
THOMAS EDWARD
ACCIDENTALLY KILLED
15th MAY 1932 AGED 24 YEARS.

Born at Blandford Street, Newcastle in 1873, Private Edward Lawson of the Gordon Highlanders became the sole Newcastle soldier to earn the prestigious VC prior to World War II. Forty-five years later he was joined by the only other Newcastle-born soldier to receive the honour, Private Adam Wakenshaw.

Posted to the Dargai Heights on India's north west frontier with Afghanistan in 1897 to deal with tribal unrest, his regiment was ordered to storm a fortified hill 'at any costs and despite all hazards'. Although twice wounded in the assault he managed to carry a badly injured comrade to safety in the face of enemy fire and then returned to rescue another. The hill was eventually captured.

Dying in 1955 aged 82, Edward was buried with full military honours at Byker and Heaton cemetery, Benton Road, Newcastle. Several years ago the Tyneside Joint Ex-Services Association organised a replacement headstone in the cemetery. At about the same time his name appeared with that of Adam Wakenshaw VC on a plaque at the junction of Westmorland Road and St James Boulevard near to both of their places of birth.

❧ *Alan Morgan*

Private Adam Herbert Wakenshaw VC

The only VC awarded to a Newcastle born soldier during the Second World War was presented posthumously in 1943 to the widow and child of Adam Herbert Wakenshaw for outstanding bravery in the Libyan Desert a year earlier.

Adam, born in 1914 and the youngest of 13 children, was a miner in civilian life. Called up at the outbreak of war into the Durham Light Infantry, he saw active service at Dunkirk before being sent to North Africa where he operated as an anti-tank gunner at Mersa Matruk.

Family of Adam Wakenshaw

During enemy action his gun crew were killed and, despite losing an arm, Adam rallied to defend the remainder of his comrades as enemy tanks approached. Initially he stemmed their advance and even set fire to one of their vehicles but suffered further injuries in the process. Adam carried on firing alone until a direct hit ended his life.

Originally buried at the battle scene alongside his gun, Adam was re-interred a year later with full military honours at El Alamein war cemetery. The remains of his 2 pounder anti-tank gun and his VC medal are displayed at the DLI Museum, Aykley Heads, near Durham city.

Recently a stained glass window has been unveiled in St Mary's RC Cathedral (where Adam was baptised and married) to celebrate his life and sacrifice to save fellow soldiers. Adam had lived most of his short life at Duke Street which stood near the road junction where Westmorland Road meets St James Boulevard. It is named Wakenshaw VC junction in honour of the hero.

Alan Morgan

Political heroes

William Henry Brockett – Gateshead's forgotten hero

William Henry Brockett, now almost a forgotten man in Gateshead, was, in Victorian times, one of the most influential political figures in the town. Without Brockett, Gateshead may not have had an MP, a dispensary or a public park and it would certainly not have had its first local newspaper *The Gateshead Observer* – arguably Brockett's most important legacy to the town.

William Henry Brockett was born in Gateshead on 23 February 1804, the fifth child of John Brockett, Clerk to the Court of Requests in Newcastle, and his wife, Frances.

By 1827, he was trading as a general commission merchant on the Sandhill Newcastle and had a private house on Gateshead High Street.

Brockett's first major political venture began in 1830 when he was one of 174 signatories who petitioned Parliament for electoral reforms. At that time Gateshead had no direct parliamentary representation. April 4 1831 saw the formation of the 'Gateshead Reform Association' with Brockett and William Kell as joint secretaries.

It was during debates surrounding parliamentary reform that Lord Londonderry famously described Gateshead as 'a vile and filthy town' and also as 'a dirty lane leading to Newcastle'. The Reform Act was eventually passed in June 1832 with Gateshead allowed to return one member to Parliament. It is no understatement to say this was due almost solely to Brockett's constant lobbying and letter writing.

Brockett then turned his attention to local politics. In 1835 he was elected to the newly formed Town Council together with his father-in-law, Thomas Wilson. In 1838, he was elected an Alderman and, in November 1839, reached the pinnacle of council achievement when elected the town's fifth mayor at the early age of 35.

Along with John Collinson, Rector of Gateshead, he was responsible for the Gateshead Dispensary, set up in 1832 as a direct result of the cholera epidemic of the previous year. He was also the prime mover in the fight against the borough holders' attempt to retain their hold on the town's common land on Windmill Hills. This victory led to the establishment of the town's first public park in 1861.

However, Brockett's lasting legacy to Gateshead was the founding of *The Gateshead Observer*. His main supporters were John George Lambton (Lord Durham) and William Hutt, Gateshead's MP from 1841.

He issued a prospectus advertising it on 1 September 1837 and the first edition appeared on 18 November 1837. It soon established itself as a paper not only of power and passion but also of integrity and repute. It consistently supported reform in the town and was a constant advocate of the people's rights and of the need for public health improvements in Gateshead.

James Clephan, the paper's main editor resigned in 1860, after which Brockett took over as editor. However, his health was already in decline and he was not able to give the paper his full attention. (It eventually ceased publication in 1886).

Brockett died on 15 January 1867 after a long illness and was buried in Gateshead East Cemetery. His grave is his most immediate memorial, recognising some of his many achievements but sadly not mentioning the *Observer*. His funeral was attended by many of the chief officials of Newcastle and Gateshead.

Anthea Lang

Joseph Cowen – champion of 'the militant democracy'

Joseph Cowen (1829-1900) was described by the *New York Times* as 'one of the most extraordinary men in Europe.'

A friend of Garibaldi and other leaders of independence movements in Italy, Poland, Hungary and Ireland, Cowen turned Tyneside into a hot bed of opposition to Europe's 19th century despotic empires.

Spies sent by foreign powers flitted in and out of Newcastle railway station trying to track Cowen's activities during the 1850s. They would have been better employed checking the loads of bricks shipped to Italy and elsewhere from Cowen's Blaydon brickworks. Inside consignments of Blaydon bricks, Cowen had hidden subversive literature and arms.

During the 1860s, Cowen took his passion for freedom to new heights, recruiting Tynesiders to go to Sicily to fight for Garibaldi, building a clandestine warship for the Poles, and pouring his energies and that of his newspaper, the *Newcastle Daily Chronicle* (parent of the present day *Evening Chronicle*), into championing the anti-slavery cause in the American Civil War.

The Cowen Memorial, Westgate Road, 1966.

But first and foremost, Cowen was a Tynesider. When he became a Member of Parliament for Newcastle in 1874 other MPs wondered if he was speaking Latin since they could not grasp his Northumbrian dialect.

Although a major employer, Cowen and his *Chronicle* keenly promoted the miners' trade unions and, in 1871, the engineers' epic strike for a nine hours working day (see Joe Wilson's song on page 147).

He helped form the first modern co-operative society in the North East at Blaydon in 1858, and he championed the right to vote for working men and women. By bringing these causes together, Cowen believed that Britain could lead the world with a fine democracy, 'the militant democracy'.

Democracy would work only if people were properly educated so Cowen revolutionised adult education by establishing Tyneside institutes that encouraged discussion and critical thinking, allowed women to take part, and even had playgrounds for the children to use while their parents were in lectures. At the Tyne Theatre and Opera House, built by Cowen in 1867, light drama, often touching on social issues, played to packed houses.

Excitement and Joe Cowen were life long companions. By urging public meetings to replace the monarchy with a republic, he prompted Queen Victoria to pull down the blinds of the royal train whenever it passed through Newcastle (see page 13 for a different version of this story). His journalists hijacked trains to be the first to get their news onto the streets through the *Chronicle*. And when he died in 1900 his funeral was one of the largest ever seen on Tyneside.

❧ Nigel Todd

Arthur Henderson, winner of the Nobel Peace Prize

Historians may debate the exact nature of Arthur Henderson's contribution to national and international politics, but, as the only old boy of Todd's Nook School on Westgate Road to win the Nobel Peace Prize, he certainly qualifies as Tyneside's finest politician. He also demonstrated a remarkable facility for finding parliamentary seats: except for three short interludes, Henderson sat in the House of Commons from 1903 until his death in 1935, during which time he lost at four General Elections and won five by-elections.

Henderson was born in Glasgow in 1863 and moved to Monday Street, Newcastle in around 1873. After school he began an apprenticeship in an iron foundry and at the age of 16 became a devout Wesleyan and abstainer. Henderson was active in his union and gained a place on Newcastle Council for Westgate North in 1892. From 1895 his political activities centred on Darlington, where he became a county councillor and the town's first Labour mayor.

As an MP, Henderson had a distinguished career. He acted as leader of the Labour Party between 1908 and 1910 and briefly in 1931. He was National Secretary from 1911-34 and had two spells as Chairman. He became a privy counsellor in 1915, served in Asquith's coalition government as President of the Board of Education and as Paymaster General, and in Lloyd George's original War Cabinet. He was appointed Home Secretary in Macdonald's administration, and was made Foreign Secretary in the second Labour Government of 1929.

Henderson's most notable achievement was on the international stage. As Foreign Secretary in 1931, he was nominated to preside over the World Disarmament Conference in Geneva in 1932. For his efforts, Henderson was awarded the Nobel Peace Prize in 1934.

Brian Bennison

Dolly Peel – anti-press-gang activist

Dolly Peel, a famous and colourful South Shields character was born Dorothy Appleby in 1782. She lived in Shadwell Street on the riverside in South Shields with her husband Cuthbert, whom she married in 1803.

Her official occupation was that of a fishwife but she was a notorious smuggler of brandy, tobacco, lace and perfume – in fact 'anything dutiable'. She was known to take and execute orders for any excisable article that might be required, smuggling up and down the North East coast from Cullercoats to Marsden Grotto and beyond. One source dubs her 'the Queen of the Smugglers'.

However, it was her determined opposition and fight against the press-gang which still stirs the imagination of all who hear her story. She is reputed to have outwitted their efforts to capture the local seamen on numerous occasions by, among other things, hiding men and boys

under her voluminous petticoats. Perhaps the most famous story tells how the press-gang, in hot pursuit of her husband, who had managed to reach their home, was kept at bay by Dolly, single-handedly, while he escaped through a window and on to the roof of their house.

When Cuthbert was eventually caught, Dolly followed him to sea, serving in the cockpit – that part of the ship where crude surgery was performed on wounded sailors – and as a powder monkey, fuelling the guns in the thick of battle. It was said that she had a nerve of iron.

There was, however, another side to this brave indefatigable woman. She was a great storyteller, about whom George B. Hodgson, *Shields Gazette* editor and author of *The Borough of South Shields* wrote, 'Had she been an educated woman she might have made a reputation as a poetess. As it was she was famous for her ability to rhyme extempore on any subject.'

Among other things, she composed an address in poetry congratulating Robert Ingham, with whom apparently she was a great favourite, on his return as the first MP for South Shields. Her song on the loss of the barque *Dove* of Sunderland, laden with Russian tallow, on the Herd Sand, enabled the 'Townenders' (as the inhabitants of the 'low end' of the town were known) to feel that the wreck was a special dispensation of Providence to help them through the hard winter of 1836.

Obviously a woman of great wit and humour she regularly entertained the crowds in South Shields Market Place, wickedly imitating the sales patter of quack doctors, while waving one of the boxes of pills they were trying to sell.

Dolly died from bronchitis at her home on 14th October 1857. She has inspired many tributes in her home town including a pub bearing her name, several oil paintings, a play (last performed at the Customs House, South Shields in 2005), a video about her life filmed on location in South Tyneside and a statue overlooking the River which was unveiled in 1987. Her great great great grandson, Reg Peel, who was largely responsible for the commissioning of the statue by Bill Gofton, continues to piece together Dolly's story with help from relatives at home and all over the world.

Although there is uncertainty about the number of children Dolly and Cuthbert had there are many who claim descent from them and, 150 years after her death, she still captivates all those who belong to her line and others besides – a daring and resourceful character and a woman ahead of her time.

Hildred Whale

Benefactors

Lord Armstrong

William Armstrong was born in Shieldfield, Newcastle, in 1810, the son of a corn merchant. He trained as a lawyer, but showed a great interest in mechanics and science. William became fascinated by the idea of harnessing the power of water and developed a plan for a hydraulic crane. In around 1845 he converted a crane on Newcastle's Quayside to water power.

The efficiency of his invention led Armstrong to leave his job as a solicitor and, in 1847, to set up a factory at Elswick for the production of his cranes and other hydraulic equipment.

The Elswick Works went on to enjoy many years of success, becoming Newcastle's largest employer. William Armstrong also branched out into arms production and shipbuilding. In the 1850s he developed a breech-loading, mobile field gun for use by artillery. Armstrong was knighted in 1859. His company went on to produce naval guns and warships, a shipyard being opened at Elswick in 1884.

In 1864, work had began on the construction of Sir William's impressive mansion, Cragside (now National Trust), situated on a hillside close to Rothbury, Northumberland. Sir William directed the planting of thousands of trees and shrubs in the extensive grounds.

In 1887, he was created 1st Baron Armstrong of Cragside. However, it is not as an arms and warship baron that he is best remembered. Lord Armstrong was also a great benefactor to his native city of Newcastle, showing generosity with his wealth. He gave his lands at

The opening of the Royal Victoria Infirmary, 11 July 1906.

Jesmond Dene and the nearby Armstrong Park to the people of the city for their enjoyment and also contributed funds towards the building of a new school for deaf children on the edge of Newcastle's Town Moor. In addition, he played a leading role in the foundation of the city's Fleming Memorial Hospital for Sick Children, and provided money for the hospital's new out-patient department.

He also gave funds for a new operating theatre and wards at the city's old Royal Infirmary, formerly known as Newcastle Infirmary, and he and Lady Armstrong helped to finance the building of Newcastle's Hancock Natural History Museum. Armstrong also contributed money towards the setting up of the city's College of Physical Science, a foundation which eventually led to the establishment of Newcastle University.

Lord Armstrong died at Cragside on December 27, 1900. He was aged 90. The inventor and philanthropist is buried in Rothbury Churchyard, near the River Coquet.

His great nephew, William Watson Armstrong, inherited his fortune. In his memory, Watson Armstrong gave £100,000 towards the fund for the building of the new Royal Victoria Infirmary in Newcastle which opened in 1906. The donation covered a third of the cost of constructing and equipping the hospital. Money created by the production of guns and warships capable of destroying life was thus by an extreme irony used to save lives and relieve suffering.

❧ *Ken Smith*

The Bubble Foundation UK

In 1991 a colleague at Granada Television asked me to help a small charity fundraising for a unit within Newcastle General Hospital. I went along to have a look, fell in love with a baby I saw there and so began my association with the charity now known as The Bubble Foundation UK.

The unit supported by the Bubble Foundation was established in Newcastle General Hospital in 1991. It treats children from all over the United Kingdom who are suffering from immune deficiency. Babies suffering from severe combined immune deficiency will die in the first year of life unless confined in a 'bubble' of sterile air. Once diagnosed they can be treated by bone marrow transplant. If this takes they will become completely healthy children. If not, they will die. The only similar unit is based in Great Ormond Street Hospital, London.

Denise Robertson with 'Bubble' children and Professor Andrew Cant at the 10th year celebration of the Bubble Foundation.

The Newcastle Unit has made amazing progress in the last few years. Its success rate in treating babies, older children and teenagers with immune deficiency is now 90% but its real triumph lies in the innovative steps it has taken to treat different serious immune disorders once thought beyond medical intervention. Graham from Liverpool is a case in point. He was admitted to the unit when he was 17. His quality of life was nil and he was resigned to an early death. Although a transplant cannot undo all previous damage it can stop further deterioration and restore quality of life. Today Graham is back in Liverpool planning a future he never thought he would see.

The unit has pioneered the use of cord blood to provide complete immunity to immune deficient children and pioneered transplant in cases of juvenile ideopathic arthritis. The results of this particular procedure are little short of miraculous.

In the past, transplants in very young children frequently failed because of lung infection and inflammation. The unit has devised new forms of treatment for both conditions which has contributed in no small measure to the raised success rates.

Lupus, a distressing condition resistant to treatment in its severest form, has responded amazingly to transplant, giving affected children a clean start. The transplant for lupus performed in the unit is believed to be the first in the world so it can be said that Newcastle is leading the way. The unit is concentrating its research and development on conditions hitherto thought untreatable. It also intends to find out why immune deficiency exists at all in some children.

Professor Cant now holds clinics in Manchester, Dublin and Edinburgh and is a leading figure in children's immunology in Europe.

Sadly, that first baby didn't survive but his brother, born a few years later, was successfully treated in the Bubble and went home to Scotland. Today he is a happy boy approaching his teens. As President of the Bubble Foundation, I am immensely proud that this amazing facility is based here in the North East. It is one more example of how we not only compete but frequently set the pace.

Denise Robertson

The People's Kitchen

Imagine yourself cold and hungry and friendless at half past eight underneath the arches of the High Level Bridge at the bottom of Dean Street on a freezing December evening. But there is something to look forward to; soon a van will arrive carrying hot soup and drinks and sandwiches as well as some people who will stop and chat for a couple of hours.

Of the many humiliating aspects of homelessness, being alone and belonging to nobody, must be worst. In 1985 Alison Kay, from Heaton, was so moved by an account of an unknown man found dead under a bush in Newcastle that she decided to do something about the problem. Co-operating with the police and Social Services she took flasks of tea and sandwiches to a pitch near the bottom of Dean Street. There she met four homeless men, and served the first of many thousands of meals. But more than just food, she offered friendship.

The word spread and soon Alison was joined by an increasing number of volunteers providing warmth, food and support. By 1994 a permanent base was needed and the Alison Centre in Bath Lane was purchased through donations. It has facilities for cooking and for storing food and clothing. Over 80 volunteers give their time cleaning, preparing and serving food, sorting clothing, driving to collect and deliver contributions and carrying out DIY repairs.

There are still around 2,000 homeless people without permanent accommodation in Newcastle. Some sleep rough on the streets; many are in temporary accommodation such as hostels. During the Kitchen's 21 years some things have changed. Initially most users were elderly, but now about 60% of people attending the Kitchen are under 25. The majority come from broken homes and have become excluded from society for different reasons. Some might be drug addicts or alcoholics, or suffer from mental illness. There are all manner of ordinary people whose lives have collapsed leaving them isolated and lonely. But, whatever the need, nobody is turned away.

Alison Kay's tradition of serving meals 'under the arches' continues. Normally

The People's Kitchen.

about 70 people turn up every Monday evening between 8.45 and 10.30pm for friendly chat, music, and in winter a warm fire. Good quality evening meals are served at the centre on Tuesday, Wednesday and Friday evenings. There is a Sunday morning 'breakfast run' at Old Eldon Square at 8.30am and Westgate Road Cemetery from 10am. On Thursday afternoons there is an open 'drop-in' session. Around 650 people visit one or other of the meal services.

The People's Kitchen has become one of Newcastle's finest symbols of humanity, respected far and wide for the warmth of its welcome to the most desperate and needy in society.

Maureen Callcott

William Turner (1761-1859), nonconformist minister

William Turner was an outstanding contributor to Newcastle life 200 years ago. He came from a family of non-conformist clergy and at just 20 years old, after university in Glasgow, he was chosen by the congregation of one of the more important Dissenting chapels in Newcastle, Hanover Square, to become its minister. The young pastor quickly made his mark, with characteristic energy, and before long had also begun to make a contribution to the life of Newcastle.

Within two years William established the first Sunday schools in the town. They taught religious instruction, reading, writing and number work and later combined to become a charity school. In 1787 he started a library at Hanover Square especially for younger members. He wrote *An Abstract of the History of the Bible*, again for younger people, as well as works on religion, civil liberty, reform and the end of slavery. He created a thriving local Tract Society whose publications were very popular with print-runs as large as 100,000. In 1809 he helped to found the (Unitarian) Auxiliary Bible Society, and was its secretary until 1831.

William did much for widows and orphans of the clergy and established a Fund for the Benefit of the Poor. In 1810 he helped to found the Royal Jubilee School 'to provide education for the children of the poor'. He was a founder of Newcastle

The Reverend William Turner.

Mechanics' Institute, its Vice-President and generous friend. He ran his own day school (1785-1803, 1813-1824), educating 210 boys in all.

William Turner is perhaps best remembered for his work leading to the foundation of the Newcastle Literary and Philosophical Society in 1793. He lectured there on about 600 occasions, on subjects as varied as chemical applications, optics, astronomy, botany, hydrostatics, electricity and mechanics. Many were influenced by his teaching, including George Stephenson.

As a concerned citizen of an overcrowded town, with poor sanitation and frequent disease, William Turner worked hard to encourage vaccination against smallpox, which was adopted in 1801; over the next 25 years more than 20,000 people were vaccinated in Newcastle. With a chemist friend he analysed local spring water to help ensure a supply of the best water in public areas.

William Turner left Hanover Square in 1841, after a ministry of almost sixty years, and moved to Manchester to live with his daughter, Anne. The president of the Newcastle Literary and Philosophical Society, Charles Bigge, praised his huge contribution to the promotion of science, literature, fine art, education and charitable causes.

This remarkable man had numerous friends from many walks of national and North Eastern life. Vigorous, hard-working, generous, public-spirited and utterly committed to the welfare of those around him, he was well-known on Tyneside and respected throughout his denomination and beyond. William Turner died in Manchester on 24 April 1859, less than three years shy of his century.

Richard Potts

Robert Spence Watson 1837-1911

Robert Spence Watson should be remembered and honoured as one of those Victorian Tynesiders whose own life improved the lives of his contemporaries of all social groups and left a legacy for future generations.

He was a Quaker, whose faith determined his efforts to improve social conditions for all, including climbing boys (chimney sweeps), trade unionists up against their employers in the courts (a solicitor, he never took fees when he acted in industrial disputes), pitmen and elementary school students (he served on the first School Boards in

Newcastle). He also founded a girls' high school, and made a major contribution to the founding of the College of Science – of which he was the first President – that was to become Newcastle University. He helped to shape the progress of Newcastle's first public library in the 1870s, serving for many years on the Library Committee. It was he who insisted upon the formation and development of the excellent Local History collection which remains probably unequalled in England. He was Secretary and then President of the Literary and Philosophical Society on Westgate Road, delivered many lectures, and wrote the first volume of its history.

He also campaigned against Britain's involvement in military conflicts from the Crimean War to the Boer War. In 1901 a mob calling for war against the Boers in South Africa threw a stone through a window of his home in Bensham Grove, Gateshead. The family kept the stone calling it 'the Free Speech Stone'. He supported political exiles from Europe, helped refugees, and was President of the Peace Society. He opposed slavery and was also President of The Friends of Russian Freedom which campaigned against the tyrannies of the Tsarist governments.

A political activist for the Liberal Party, in 1907 he was made a Privy Councillor. Although he accepted such offices he refused offers of a safe parliamentary seat, convinced that the right course was to avoid the pursuit of personal ambition.

All manner of visitors, humble, famous and infamous were regularly welcomed to his home. His wife Elizabeth was a partner in his public work when their six children were grown up, and a contributor to local social improvement in her own right. She also shared his love of mountaineering in Norway and the Alps, where, on their honeymoon, they pioneered a new route.

Bensham Grove remains a significant asset to Gateshead life. On Elizabeth's death in 1919 the house became a community centre of learning known as The Bensham Settlement. By the late 1940s it was struggling to be self-supporting so was taken over by Gateshead Council and it continues to this day to be fully used for the purposes for which the Spence Watsons left it.

Maureen Callcott

Sporting Heroes

Tom Graveney, cricketer

If you want to make the eyes of a cricket lover of a certain age go slightly moist, just mention Tom Graveney. They will go off into a trance as they think about his 47,793 first class runs (4,882 of them for England) and his 122 centuries which make him one of the most successful batsmen of all time. But it's not just the quantity of runs he scored but the way he did it, because Tom was one of the most elegant and stylish batsmen ever seen.

What many people do not know is that Tom started his life on the banks of the Tyne and benefited from the local water. He was born in Riding Mill in 1927, moved to Newcastle and, after a couple of years at school, moved with his mother to the South West where he acquired the accent that made his television commentaries almost as enjoyable as his batting. Tom began his career as a cricketer, as an alternative to continuing his life in the army, with Gloucestershire in 1948 and after 296 appearances he moved to Worcestershire in 1961, where he played another 208 times before retiring in 1970.

Tom's contribution to cricket has been considerable, but what has made him a great Tynesider is his legacy to the region. We have had the odd success up here. Heavy industry has come and gone, a football team has its odd moment of glory, however Tom helped to leave something for those that wanted to follow in his footsteps. As Durham bid for first class status they needed credibility and that West Country

accent came to help them. He presented their promotional video, advised them on what to do and his presence reminded people that the North East could produce top cricketers.

Cricket has boomed since then. Not only are Durham playing in the first division of the County Championship and three players are representing England but the effect has rippled down, and on a summer Sunday hundreds of children are playing in competitions that weren't around 15 years ago. Tom meanwhile is enjoying his retirement. In 2005 he became the first professional cricketer to become president of the MCC and anyone who heard him during one of his many engagements that year, or just chatted to him, will know that he has not lost his love of cricket or the North East.

Ian Jackson

Jackie Milburn 1924-1988 – Wor Jackie

To the people of Tyneside he was known as 'Wor Jackie' and when Jackie Milburn died on 9 October 1988 over 30,000 mourners lined the streets as his funeral cortège passed through Newcastle on its way to St Nicholas' Cathedral. During his years with Newcastle United (1943-1957), he made 397 appearances and scored 200 goals – a club record broken by Alan Shearer in 2006. Jackie won three FA Cup medals with Newcastle and was awarded 13 England caps. However he was always something more than a great footballer to Tynesiders who awarded him iconic status. What is more, he deserved it: he did not have feet of clay inside his football boots.

Jackie Milburn was born in Ashington on 11 May 1924 and, like many of his contemporaries, he went to work down the pit. He played football in his spare time and was given a trial by Newcastle United in 1943. The story goes that he ate two pies sitting on the steps of St James' Park before reporting for his trial match, in which he scored six goals. Within 48 hours he had signed to join United. As a player, Milburn had speed and packed a very good shot. During his early years with Newcastle he played on the wing or as an inside forward. However, in the 1947-48 season the Newcastle manager, George Martin, switched him to centre forward and in his first game in this position he scored a hat trick. He went on to make the number 9 shirt his own. But Milburn was not only a fine footballer, he was also a scrupulously clean player and his private life was untouched by scandal. He was an outstanding role model.

In 1957 he severed his connections with Newcastle United to join the Irish League club Linfield as player-manager. At his new club he played in the European Cup competition, won an Irish Cup medal, and was voted Ulster Footballer of the Year in 1958. After this he was briefly player-manager of the southern non-league Yiewsley Town, and then succeeded Alf Ramsey as manager of Ipswich. Unfortunately,

NEWCASTLE UNITED A.F.C. CUP FINALISTS, 1951-52
R. Cowell, J. Harvey (Capt.), R. Simpson, F. Brennan, A. McMichael, E. Robledo,
T. Walker, W. Foulkes, J. Milburn, G. Robledo, R. Mitchell.

Newcastle United's winning team, Jackie Milburn centre of the front row, which beat Arsenal 1-0 with a George Robledo goal in the FA Cup Final on 3 May 1952.

Jackie was not cut out to be a manager and after 18 months in the job he returned to his native North East where he got a job as a sports journalist. He was not forgotten by Newcastle's fans and in 1967 he was given a testimonial match at St James' Park that attracted a crowd of 45,000. A bronze statue of Jackie Milburn was erected in Northumberland Street in 1991 and eight years later it was moved to St James' Boulevard, close to the ground where he had scored so many memorable goals.

Archie Potts

Police Horse Paris

You probably know the old chestnut about who played cup finals at Wembley in successive weeks but have you heard of the grey gelding with 1,000 league appearances? Police Horse Paris, an Irish draught horse known to his stable mates as Chubby, retired in 2006 after a long career during which he not only kept order at football grounds but undertook other crowd control duties and took part in ceremonies as the mount of Sgt David Roythorne, head of Northumbria police's mounted section.

Chubby was born in Ireland and came to Tyneside via a dealer in Scotland when he was six. When choosing a horse the police look for a strong, healthy animal, but they also examine its temperament. It seems they selected the ideal horse in Chubby who turned out to be 'as brave as a lion but as placid as a lamb' says Sgt Roythorne. He was then trained using the tried and tested methods of repetition and reward which never stopped during his working life.

Sgt Roythorne met Chubby when he took over as head of the Mounted Police section after 19 years with the CID. It was the perfect job for a keen horseman and he now manages the nine horses at Kirkley Hall and their support. Together they have become a much loved attraction at ceremonies, fetes and Remembrance Day parades. One of the highlights was a trip to Windsor Castle to take part in All the Queen's Horses.

Now aged 24, Chubby is a pensioner. He retired after Alan Shearer's testimonial game on 11 May 2006 and was sent to a farm in Northumberland on permanent loan. Dave Roythorne thinks he will miss work but will soon take to retirement. He is gregarious and his favourite hobby is eating, so there should be no regrets about hanging up his stirrups.

The old team won't loose touch. There will be visits to Chubby's new home and in the meantime Dave will be training a replacement and trying to think up a name for the student. All Northumbria police horses have a name starting with a P so as they have been in existence for 100 years suitable names are running short. One thing is certain though, no matter how long there are police horses there will never be another Chubby.

ßö *Ian Jackson*

Northumbria Police

Another famous sports personality, Newcastle United's Alan Shearer with Chubby.

Anna Flowers

Footballing hero Alan Shearer's own retirement was marked by wrapping Grey's Monument in the Newcastle United black and white colours on 12 May 2006.

Renforth poses at the height of his fame.

James Renforth was born on 7th April 1842 in New Pandon Street, Newcastle. His father was an anchorsmith and James found employment as a smith's striker, hammering lumps of hot metal into shape. After an adventurous, and under age, foray to India with the relief force to put down the Indian Mutiny in 1857, Renforth began his professional rowing career on the Tyne in 1866.

He won two single sculling races against other novices in that year and by the autumn of 1867, when he defeated both of the Boyd brothers, he appeared to have a bright future ahead of him. The problem he faced was that his performances were so impressive that nobody was keen to throw their money away by putting up a stake against such a rapidly improving sculler.

Renforth went round the regattas in 1868, competing for prize money which was small in comparison to the stakes for a big head-to-head race. His victory in the single sculls race at the Thames Regatta of 1868 changed everything. The champion, Harry Kelley, was forced to consider a challenge from Renforth. The medium rank scullers who had been avoiding Renforth had been bypassed.

Renforth was still a comparative novice, having had only one head-to-head contest in a skiff; all his other match victories were in open boats which were shorter, beamier craft. His challenge to Kelley was accepted and they raced on the Thames, over the Putney to Mortlake course, in November 1868. Renforth took the lead and held off Kelley, while rowing well within himself, to win by four lengths. It was a great victory but was disastrous for Renforth's chances of securing another big money match. He was the Champion of the Tyne, of the Thames, of England, and, by virtue of earlier victories over foreign oarsmen by Kelley and Chambers, of the World, but the titles were never to be defended. Renforth was so feared as a sculler that no challenger could be found.

Renforth switched to rowing as the stroke oar of a four and enjoyed enormous success leading the Tyne Champion Four. It was while stroking the champion four that he collapsed during a race defending the four-oared championship of the world in St. John, New Brunswick, Canada on 23rd August 1871. A few hours later he was dead. Renforth was buried in Gateshead on the 10th September 1871 with 100,000 people attending the funeral.

So why do I think James Renforth is Tyneside's finest rower and not, say the much better known Harry Clasper? In a nutshell, which it has to be, Renforth died as undefeated sculling Champion of the World, unable to attract a serious challenge in three years because he was so feared, while Clasper, despite his undoubted abilities, never even won the sculling championship of the Thames.

Ian Whitehead

Colin Veitch – Tyneside's finest footballer

In my opinion Tyneside's finest footballer played for Newcastle United during the club's Edwardian heyday of three championships and five cup finals between 1905 and 1911. Colin Veitch made over 300 appearances in nine different positions, captained the side and was capped by England. He was also prominent in the players' union, had a brief spell as a football club manager and longer employment as a sports journalist. Away from football, Veitch was both performer and musical director with an operatic society, conducted choirs and was a founder of Newcastle's Peoples' Theatre, where he acted, produced and wrote pantomimes.

Veitch was born on Byker Bank in 1881. He came from an enlightened and strongly socialist family. After captaining Newcastle Boys in 1895 it seemed likely that he would succeed as a professional footballer, although at the time he was actively contemplating an academic career. He signed indentures as student teacher at Heaton's North View School a year before making his Newcastle United debut as an amateur against Heart of Midlothian in 1899. For the first few years of his paid career he continued to attend Armstrong College.

From 1902 Veitch became a important member of the Newcastle United first team, usually as a half-back or centre-half. His days as captain and first-team regular were coming to an end by the time he assumed office as chairman of the players' union in 1911. After war service in France, Veitch joined the coaching staff at St James' Park and

Colin Veitch, second from the left, front row, at Newcastle United's ground in 1905.

established the Newcastle Swifts nursery team. When he was unceremoniously sacked as a cost-cutting measure in 1926, he joined Bradford City as manager. Three years later he became a journalist with the *Newcastle Evening Chronicle*.

When Veitch died in a Swiss sanatorium in 1938, the Manchester Guardian said his name had been 'synonymous with honesty and good fellowship'. In interviews during his playing days, and later in journalism, Veitch demonstrated an instinct for honour and fair play, stressing the comradeship that the game provided. At times his attitude appeared that of an innocent abroad in football, some kind of displaced, gifted amateur of Corinthian spirit. But the same man was credited with inventing strategies which forced reform of the offside law; he introduced deceptive dummying at free kicks; was first to use a blackboard to explain tactics to team mates and then, as a manager, engaged an overseas athletics coach.

The impressive statistics of Veitch's playing career qualify him as an extraordinary footballer, but his greatness was in the manner in which he managed to straddle two cultures. He steadfastly stuck to the older values of conviviality and courtesy whilst pursuing a more calculating, methodical approach to the game. Colin Veitch was both the gentleman and the player.

❧ Brian Bennison

Tyneside's finest boxer – Seaman Tommy Watson (1908-71)

The inter-war years were something of a golden age for boxing in Britain: there were many good boxers competing for a place on fight bills and boxing matches attracted large crowds. On Tyneside – especially during the depression years – there were hundreds of young men who entered the professional ranks in order to earn a few extra bob and those boxers who aspired to a championship fight had to battle their way through a long list of rival contenders. Boxing titles were highly valued and difficult to win. The only Geordie to win a British title in this period and earn the right to fight for a world title was Seaman Tommy Watson. He fought the leading boxers of his time and lost only nine fights in his entire career.

Tommy Watson and his wife, Kitty.

Born on 2 June 1908 in Scotswood and brought up in Byker, Tommy Watson joined the Royal Navy at the age of 16 and soon made his mark in service boxing, before turning professional in the following year. Six years and 89 fights later, he travelled to Merseyside where he defeated the local idol, Nel Tarleton, to win the British featherweight title. Six months after this Watson fought a Cuban called Eligio Sardinas for the World featherweight title at Madison Square Gardens in New York. Sardinas, who fought under the ring name Kid Chocolate, retained his title after 15 gruelling rounds. Watson had lost to a great champion and although there was talk of a return bout this never took place. Instead Watson successfully defended his British title against Johnny McMillan in Glasgow, before losing it back to Nel Tarleton. Moving up into the lightweights Watson became a leading contender for the British lightweight title, then held by Kid Berg, but was forced to retire with a cut eye in a final eliminating bout with George Daly. Tommy Watson then retired, after 121 professional bouts, to become a publican and boxing referee. He died on 27 January 1971, a highly respected member of the boxing fraternity.

Archie Potts

Unsung Heroes

The fisherwives

Fisherwives endured arduous lives. Winter and summer, in fair weather and foul, their day began by prising mussels off the rocks: around 800 were needed for bait. Their long skirts hoisted as high as decency permitted, it was back-breaking work, slippery underfoot, with regular soakings from the chilly waters of the North Sea.

It was a fisherwife's job to untangle, clean, re-bait and re-furl the lines. Each mussel had to be 'skairned' (opened) and the meat removed. Lines were about 400 yards long; from them hung cords fitted with barbed hooks. Skilled in the task of baiting and furling the lines so they would run out smoothly from the boat, it was a matter of competitive pride that the line you prepared should allow your man to catch a fish on every hook. Fisherwives needed sharp eyesight and nimble fingers for baiting – fingers jabbed on those vicious hooks turned septic and often had to be removed.

The women also had their normal household tasks: baking bread, childcare, house-cleaning and laundering. Whilst their menfolk were at sea, spare moments saw them knitting a gansey (sweater) in the pattern particular to their husband's family or making stockings for themselves or the children. They'd work on the proggy mats for floor coverings or cut down a pair of old trousers for one of their growing lads. However, when the boats came in, it was straight down to the shore to help haul them up onto the beach. The men would weight down the stern end so that the women, up to their waists in seawater, could insert the wheels beneath the bow and the whole boat [coble], with its cargo of fish, was then rolled ashore. There was more work in early July, when the herring shoals were running. They gutted the fish and hawked it round the streets crying 'Caller Herrin'' to alert local households of their wares.

The worst of times came when a ship was dashed upon the rocks. All the fisherfolk waded into the sea attempting to rescue survivors. Picture the awful scene: black night, howling wind, huge waves crashing shorewards, sand scouring the skin, spray blinding the eyes, and the knowledge that out there souls were drowning and that in another place and time it could be their own husbands and sons needing rescue from fisherfolk just like them.

Oh yes, let's cheer those fisherwives: heroines every one.

Maureen Brook

Fisherwomen posed at North Shields for photographer Edgar G. Lee around 1898.

Tyneside's finest? … Your Mam of course!

This is intended as a tribute to ALL our Mams; everyone has one, and on Tyneside we have the best in the business.

Ron French

One of the finest, Ron's mother, a Geordie Mam.

My own particular Mam, Eleanor, (1903-1994) was a Byker Lass, born in Graham Street into a world less complicated than today: tram cars and pony and trap rides down to the coast, through cornfields 'all the way' from Heaton to Cullercoats. She had landed in a world where the Wright Brother's feats were still six months in the future and Tyneside author Jack Common was being born just around the corner.

Her father, a ship's carpenter, was often away on long voyages, so young Eleanor's greatest influence was her own Mam who gave her a simple, truthful chapel-going upbringing that made her the person she would be for the rest of her life.

Her book prizes for exemplary attendance at chapel and Chillingham Road School in Heaton, included her Methodist Hymnal, still treasured today.

Losing her parents before she was 21, she saw two World Wars with rationing, Spanish influenza, the General Strike and the dole shaping the frugal period between them.

During World War One she worked at Mr Leventhal's 'Penny Bazaar' and Gamble's fruiterers. By 1919 she was a tea-blender and packer at 'Tommy Bells' (the Bero Flour people) in Bath Lane. As she made her way home after work each day, her paths crossed with the young Teddy French, heading for home in Stowell Street after a day at the Naval Yard.

Both were choir members at the Central Hall at the 'Big Lamp' on Westgate Road and their courtship led to a long and happy marriage. After the two-day honeymoon at Shotley Bridge, they returned on the little steam train and were amazed at the 'turn-out' at Central Station: for a short while they thought it was for them, only to discover that United were arriving home from Wembley with the cup that day!

The family moved to Hebburn in 1925 where Eleanor supported her husband in his local politics. They looked forward all year to a week's self-catering holiday in Alston, Cumbria. Eleanor would live to see man land on the moon and to meet the Queen. Her family grew to include seven grandchildren and four great-grandchildren. We remember her gentle qualities and love and affection she gave so simply to so many; you always felt uplifted after a visit to see her. Her humanity and common sense bridged a gap to make friends of all ages. We were so lucky to have her.

❧ Ron French

The miner's wife

" Aa was just taking the bairn doon the doctor's, for her cough like, when the pit siren sounded. Well, me blood froze. Wor Tommy was on shift that morning – he's a drawer which means taking out the supports put up the day before, and Aa knew from what he'd said the night before they were being cautious because they'd heard ominous noises off and on all day. Anyway, Aa picked up the bairn and, even though Aa was expecting, Aa fairly flew doon to the pit yard, wi' aall the other pitmen's wives who were streaming in, faces tight and strained as they waited to hear what was gannin' on. We aall huddled together, wondering, worried.

We'd been there awhile before the deputy came out and told wus that there'd been a fall of rock inside the seam they were working on. My heart lurched and Aa clutched wor Patsy so hard she began to bubble. Betsy Armstrong from next door took her from us and comforted her. Betsy's got six of her own, so knaas what she's deein'. Her man and her lad, Bobby, were on back shift, she was just there to help. We waited and waited. Ee, Aa was so scared Aa thought me insides had turned to waater.

In the end they got all of them out. There were broken bones and head injuries, but just one death – Tommy, my man.

The insurance policy paid for a good funeral – black horses with plumes – and aal the pitmen who were off shift walked behind the hearse. While we were at the cemetery, the wives went in and made tea and sandwiches: it was a good wake.

The coal company gave me a smidgeon of pension, not enough to keep wus. The house on Colliery Raa was theirs too so Aa had to move out and gan back to me Mam and Dad's. Ee, Aa missed me man, and Patsy missed her Da, Then the new bairn – Hazel – was born and took away some of the sorrow. The other wives were good too. When I got a job to pay wor way, they'd take my bairns out with aall the others for a picnic day on the beach. They'd have their bottle of pop and jam sandwiches and run around and make sand-castles like the rest.

Not the life Aa'd planned, but we managed fine."

❧ *Maureen Brook*

Women, some apparently relieved, await news at the scene of the Benwell Montagu Pit disaster of 30 March 1925, when 38 men and boys died.

Inventors and Entrepreneurs

Tyneside is spoilt for choice when it comes to inventors. Take your pick from Lord Armstrong and his hydraulic machinery and rifled artillery barrel, Charles Parsons and his steam turbine, Joseph Swan and his electric light bulb, Henry Greathead and William Wouldhave and their lifeboat and the combined genius of railway pioneers George and Robert Stephenson.

There was even North Shields-born William Harbutt, an art teacher who invented plasticine and Newcastle's Arthur George, who patented the aircraft joystick.

Tony Henderson

Tyneside has long proved to be a fruitful laboratory for inventors such as William Lord Armstrong and his hydraulic machinery, Thomas Sopwith and his 'Monocleid Writing Cabinet', Joseph Wilson Swan and his electric filament lamp, and William Woodger who 'invented' the Kippered Herring, better known now simply as the 'kipper', at his curing house near the end of Newcastle's High Level Bridge; had there been a section in this book for Tyneside's finest contributor to the English breakfast, he would probably have been the only candidate. Many of the inventions of people such as these were important in their time, but were overtaken by subsequent developments. For example Hugh Lee Pattinson's new method for desilverising lead, first developed at Blaydon on Tyne in 1833, eventually gave way to the Parkes Process of 1850 and the Rozan Process of 1871.

Stafford M. Linsley

Gladstone Adams

Perhaps the finest inventor of them all is Gladstone Adams, who ran a photography business in Station Road, Whitley Bay. His invention had everything to do with an experience which would become all too familiar for present-day generations of Newcastle United supporters. In April, 1908 he made the then epic trip by car from Newcastle to London to watch United lose the FA Cup Final to Wolves. The long grind back North was not helped as he had to stop constantly to clear snow from the windscreen.

Gladstone Adams' windscreen wipers preserved in Newcastle's Discovery Museum.

The pain of defeat was eased by his vision of the windscreen wiper. He took his wooden model of the windscreen wiper to the Motor Show in 1911 and it was patented a year later. It is now used in all forms of transport around the world.

The model is now in the keeping of Newcastle's Discovery Museum.

Gladstone went on to serve as a captain in the Royal Flying Corps in the First World War and helped arrange the funeral of the German ace the Red Baron.

But what probably meant more to him than anything is that he became Newcastle United's official photographer.

&⁊ *Tony Henderson*

When Gladstone Adams was not out photographing footballers he made a living photographing fairies!

William Armstrong – Tyneside's Finest Industrialist

Lord Armstrong's statue outside the Hancock Museum, Great North Road.

In a once heavily industrialised area such as Tyneside, it should be no simple task to select one individual as the 'finest' person to have been involved in the creation, ownership and management of an industrial undertaking, but William George (Lord) Armstrong (1810-1900) stands out above all others. Not only did he create a huge industrial empire, and in so doing indirectly changed the face of the west end of Newcastle, but he was also a great benefactor to the city of Newcastle and an influential figure throughout many parts of the world. None of this was foreseen when Armstrong began his small factory on a narrow strip of land between the river and the railway at Elswick in the 1840s.

Although he began his career as a lawyer, Armstrong never quite abandoned his early ideas for mechanical and electrical devices. His ideas on hydraulic machinery led him to establish the Newcastle Cranage Company in 1846, with a commission to build hydraulic cranes on Newcastle's quayside. Messrs W.G. Armstrong & Co. was formed early in the following year and the production of hydraulic machinery began immediately with a workforce of 20 to 30 men; by 1852, with several important contracts completed, the workforce had grown to 352.

Hydraulic devices, including cranes and swing bridges, continued to be made at Elswick for the rest of Armstrong's life and after, but the Crimean War provided the impetus for a new product – armaments. The Elswick Ordnance Factory was founded in January 1859 to supply the government with Armstrong guns. Soon orders for guns flowed in from Italy, Egypt, Turkey, Russia, Austria, Denmark, Holland, Chile and Peru. The company diversified into the manufacture of naval guns which were supplied to navies throughout the world.

When the Swing Bridge was officially opened in 1876, it was the largest of its kind in the world. The Italian vessel *Europa* was the first to pass the new bridge on its way to the Elswick works where the largest hydraulic shear legs in the world loaded the largest gun ever built. On Europa's return to Italy, the gun was unloaded by the largest hydraulic crane in the world. All except the ship itself had been designed and built at Elswick.

For many years it had been Armstrong's practice to sleep in a factory office to deal with any problems which might arise on the night shift, but from about 1875, he lived almost permanently at Cragside, Rothbury, devoting much of his time to developing the house and gardens, and to entertaining important guests. By 1892, when Armstrong made his last appearance at the Elswick works, 13,000 men were employed there. When he commenced his works, the west end of Newcastle was essentially rural; now it was covered with rows of houses, in large part providing accommodation for workers at Armstrong's factory.

⊱ Stafford M. Linsley

Armstrong's Elswick works around 1870.

Richard Grainger was not an architect in the technical sense of the word but he had an unparalleled eye for architectural beauty. Through his associations with architects such as John Dobson, Thomas Oliver and John Wardle he developed central Newcastle into the fine city it is today.

Grainger was born in High Friar Lane in 1798. His father died when Richard was young so he grew up with his mother, brother and sister in a two bedroom tenement in a poor area of town. His mother did her best to give the family an education and a healthy childhood under harsh circumstances.

On completing school Grainger was apprenticed to a carpenter/builder – when Grainger became a successful developer he employed his former master! As a teenager Grainger was known for his 'power of mind and comprehensiveness of understanding far above the common'.

His first undertaking was the building of Higham Place (designed by Thomas Oliver) in 1819/20. Large scale building projects followed including Blackett Street and Leazes Terrace (again by Thomas Oliver) in the 1820s. In 1831 building began on the Royal Arcade at the lower end of Pilgrim Street and this marked the start of a long and fruitful association with John Dobson.

A public dinner was held in the Assembly Rooms in 1833 to honour Richard Grainger, who was presented with with a silver tureen and salver together with a portrait. By now his plans were becoming so grand that it was necessary for Grainger to develop an association with Town Clerk John Clayton to gain Council support. His proposals included a magnificent street to join Dean Street to Blackett Street. This development meant the removal of relatively new markets from

the site. Approval was duly given and the news was reportedly greeted by peals from the churches, bonfires and other rejoicings. The street was originally named Upper Dean Street but its name was soon changed to Grey Street.

Grainger's developments included Eldon Square, the Grainger Market, the Theatre Royal and much of the area known today as Grainger Town. He led a workforce of up to 2000 men who, although he was a hard taskmaster (resisting several strikes), are said to have held him in high regard. Grainger and his wife Rachael had 15 children.

Jack and John Leslie

Richard Grainger, builder and businessman.

Thomas Elliot Harrison – Tyneside's finest civil engineer

The name of Stephenson is understandably linked with railway engineering, both nationally and locally. In the North East, however, another engineer was responsible for the major part of the construction and operation of railways in the middle years of the 19th century; Thomas Elliot Harrison (1808-1888). He was born in Fulham, London, on 4 April 1808 but came to live in the North East as a child. He was eventually employed by Robert Stephenson as a surveyor for the proposed London & Birmingham Railway.

Under Stephenson, Harrison became resident engineer for the Newcastle & Berwick Railway (for which he undertook the greater part of the design work) and was instructed by the directors to prepare plans 'for the whole of the bridges including those across the Tyne and the Tweed.' He then became the railway's chief engineer and general manager and was involved in the formation of the North Eastern Railway (NER), created by amalgamation in 1854. He subsequently initiated the expansion of the railway until it was described as 'the most complete monopoly in the United Kingdom.'

With Stephenson, he had been responsible for the layout of the Newcastle Central Station and many other buildings including stations at Leeds and York. He was also involved in dock construction, including the 50 acre Tyne Dock at Jarrow which 'shipped more coal than any other dock in the world'.

Harrison married Margaret Adair White of Whitburn, in 1834 and then Sophia Jane Collinson in 1859. He lived in Whitburn for around 40 years and died there of heart failure on 20 March 1888, having been at work on the day before his death.

Harrison, dubbed 'Honest Tom', was President of the Institution of Civil Engineers in 1873. Under his guidance the NER came to occupy a position of great strength in the Northumberland and Durham coal trade. In spite of this he is little known and is commemorated only by a very modest plaque on the High Level Bridge which notes his involvement and that of Robert Stephenson.

Robert W. Rennison

Charles Parsons – the floating inventor

Charles Parsons, Tyneside-based inventor of the steam turbine engine, was the son of the Third Earl of Rosse, a noted astronomer. Charles was born in London in 1854 but brought up at his family's ancestral home in County Offally, Ireland.

As a boy, Charles took sea trips in his father's yachts. He went on to attend Trinity College, Dublin, and later Cambridge University where he achieved high honours in mathematics. While at Cambridge he was an enthusiastic member of a rowing crew.

In 1877, Charles Parsons joined the Elswick Works of W.G. Armstrong in Newcastle as a 'premium' apprentice. At the beginning of 1884, he became a junior partner with ship equipment manufacturer Clarke Chapman & Co, of Gateshead.

Charles now took one of the most significant steps in his career by inventing a steam turbine engine for driving a dynamo to generate elec-

Charles Parsons, 'the Chief', stands beside the cab on Turbinia, from where he controlled the engines.

tricity. It was a technological leap forward of the highest order. Clarke Chapman began manufacturing these steam turbo-generators to provide electric lighting for ships.

In 1889, Charles, together with friends, formed a company, C.A. Parsons & Co., which set up a works at Heaton, Newcastle, and further developed and expanded the production of turbo-generators. These land-based turbines sparked a revolution which led to the cheap and efficient production of electricity worldwide.

However, Charles also pressed ahead with a project to apply his invention to ships. In 1893-94 he developed a boat to test and demonstrate the advantages of the steam turbine engine at sea. The boat, launched into the Tyne at Wallsend in 1894, was named *Turbinia*. Fitted with turbines, she became the world's fastest vessel. Charles sailed out of the Tyne aboard her on many test runs in the North Sea. In 1897, at the Fleet Review in Spithead, *Turbinia*, with Parsons at the engine room controls, staged a spectacular display of speed, clocking up 34.5 knots.

This publicity stunt proved a great success and the world's first turbine-driven warship, the torpedo-boat destroyer HMS *Viper*, was launched on the Tyne in 1899. The year 1907 saw the Tyne's most famous passenger liner, *Mauretania*, sail on her maiden voyage across the Atlantic equipped with giant turbine engines which made her a speed queen.

Charles Parsons received numerous honours. In 1911 he was knighted and in 1927 was awarded the Order of Merit. He died, aged 77, in 1931 while on a cruise. He is buried, alongside his wife Katherine, in Kirkwhelpington Churchyard, Northumberland.

Ken Smith

Walter Scott was born on 17 August 1826 at Holm Cultram, near Silloth, Cumberland, and after attending the village school was apprenticed as a stonemason. Aged 23 he established himself as a builder in Newcastle. Early major contracts were warehouses at Sunderland and Tyne Dock, together with the portico of the Central Station; one of his first railway-building contracts was a branch line to Newcastle Quayside.

Among Scott's contracts were St Nicholas's mental hospital, the masonry approaches of the first Redheugh bridge, the Byker and Glasshouse bridges in Newcastle and docks at Burntisland, Ayr, the Hartlepools and Silloth. He built a new quay wall for the Newcastle Corporation and was eventually taking on contracts valued at half a million pounds. In 1884 the firm made its first major venture into water supply with the construction of reservoirs at Hury (completed 1892) and Blackton (1896), both for the Stockton and Middlesbrough Water Board.

During the decade beginning in 1885 he duplicated the railway northwards from the Central Station to Heaton, work which included the Dean Street arch and Ouseburn and Willington viaducts. He built major extensions to the Station, Douglas and County hotels. In 1887 he began work on the City and South London Underground, 'the world's first deep-level electric railway'; it was followed by several similar contracts and by 1893 his work focused on railway contracts nationwide – of up to a million pounds each – rather than its earlier emphasis on building work based on Tyneside.

In 1880 Scott purchased three collieries in county Durham; in 1882 he became the owner of the Tyne Publishing Company Ltd at Felling; in 1885 he became a shipowner; and three years later he took over a steelworks at Leeds. Other investments followed and he became a director or partner of some 20 companies. Additionally, he was Councillor for Newcastle's Elswick Ward and from 1901 was a magistrate for Northumberland.

Scott married twice, with six sons and two daughters resulting from his first marriage. From about 1880 he lived in Bentinck House in Benwell but later he acquired an additional country residence, Beauclerc, at Riding Mill. In 1907 he was created baronet. He died in France on 8 April 1910. He was unusual in the breadth of his interests and, in all, he provided employment for a staff of possibly 7,000 men: 2,500 of them in contracting and 4,500 in mining and steel. In spite of his success, however, he remains almost unknown.

Robert W. Rennison

George and Robert Stephenson – revolutionary father and son

George Stephenson 1781-1848.

Tyneside locomotive engineers George Stephenson and his son, Robert, were key players in the revolution which led to the spread of steam railways across the globe.

George was born at Wylam in 1781, the son of a colliery workman. At the age of 14, he became an assistant fireman at a pit and later began to display a great talent for repairing machinery.

He married Frances Henderson in 1802 and the couple moved to a cottage at Willington Quay where George had obtained a job. The couple's son, Robert, was born at Willington Quay in 1803.

In 1812 George Stephenson's talent for mechanics was recognised when he was appointed enginewright at Killingworth Colliery. In 1814 he constructed his first steam locomotive which he named *My Lord* (or possibly *Blucher*) and which ran on iron rails. In July of that year the engine was successfully put into operation on the Killingworth Waggonway, which ran close to George's Dial Cottage at West Moor. George went on to build 15 more locomotives at Killingworth.

In 1815, he invented his famous miner's safety lamp, known affectionately as the 'Geordie', which proved a superb gas detector and saved many pitmen's lives.

George was clearly a man of great energy, for in 1819 he began directing the laying of a new railway for Hetton Colliery in County Durham. Part of this line was operated by three of his locomotives.

George went on to plan and direct the building of the Stockton and

Robert Stephenson 1803-1859.

Darlington Railway, the first public railway in the world to use steam locomotives. This line opened in 1825 using engines built at the world's first locomotive factory, situated in Newcastle. The factory had been opened by George, Robert, and two partners. The first engines produced for the new railway were *Locomotion* and *Hope*.

George was also to direct the building of the Liverpool and Manchester Railway, which became the world's first public line, carrying passengers as well as freight, operated entirely by steam locomotives. It opened in 1830. The engines for this line, including the famous *Rocket*, were also built at the Newcastle works, their construction being masterminded by Robert, a locomotive engineer of undoubted brilliance. Robert also achieved renown as a designer of great bridges, including the magnificent High Level Bridge across the Tyne, opened in 1849.

George died in 1848 and Robert in 1859. Curiously, neither is buried on Tyneside. Robert lies at rest in Westminster Abbey, far from his native river. George is buried in Chesterfield, Derbyshire, where he lived during his last years. He has the distinction of being the only pit workman to appear on the back of a £5 note; a remarkable achievement.

❧ *Ken Smith*

George Stephenson – hero, inventor, engineer

When I was first asked to write my 'Finest' nomination for this book, I felt rather honoured and, at the time, foolishly thought, 'That'll be easy'. How wrong could I have been?

It's not until you sit down that you actually realise what a difficult task it is to choose your favourite street, view, invention, hero, drink, (that one's easy, vodka), building, ship, ruin, engineer, sportsperson, area or landscape.

As I could only choose one, I came up with a rather novel, crafty plan. What if I could combine more than one category with a single nomination. So, I sat and thought, and I sat and thought, then I considered and then I contemplated. At one stage I even contemplated deliberating, but soon went off the idea on time grounds.

What if, I thought to myself, I could narrow it down to someone who was a hero, an inventor and an engineer? If I could, then only one person would possibly fit that bill – George Stephenson – so he is my nomination.

Of course everyone has heard of George Stephenson, he was something to do with railways wasn't he? He has a school named after him in Killingworth. But do we honestly realise what this man did, not only for the North East, but the entire world?

From an early age, George showed all the makings of an engineer. He was constantly fascinated by machines and after joining his father down the pit, would dismantle colliery engines, just to see how they worked. A typical young lad, but this young lad was different. He had vision.

I do wonder if that vision allowed Stephenson to foresee that his ground-breaking rail system would change the size of our world forever? In essence it would shrink nation and continent and enable people to see places, countries, wonders, they'd previously only heard or read about. It was something so unique that it touched the lives of billions of human beings.

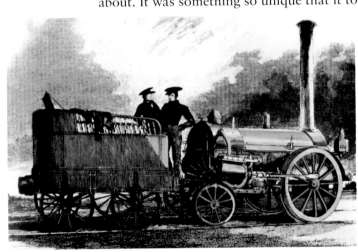

George Stephenson was a visionary, he was a hero, an inventor and an engineer and the best bit is, he was from the North East. What a message for the rest of world.

Paul Wappat

Stephenson's Northumbrian engine.

Locomotion, photographed in 1916 against an added backdrop. It was displayed at Darlington Bank Top station for many years.

George Stephenson – engineer with vision

As a mechanical engineering undergraduate in the late 1950s, I was asked by a lecturer to state the primary function of an engineer in society. After providing several highfalutin answers he cut me short and announced that 'The primary function of an engineer in society is to avoid work'. He was correct of course, but great engineers also need an unswerving conviction in the ultimate triumph of their plan in order to convince a sceptical and frequently conservative public of its merits.

George Stephenson invented neither the steam locomotive, nor the track on which it ran, but he had the foresight to see that railways could do so much more than simply carry minerals from their source to the nearest port or navigable river. He believed that he and other hand-picked railway engineers, including his son Robert, could bring about a more widespread revolution in inland transport; he also possessed the inherent stubbornness necessary to bring that dream to fruition. As he wrote to a friend, 'I will send the locomotive as the great Missionary over the World', and the extent to which he succeeded can be seen in the world's railway systems – in large measure George Stephenson's handwriting on the landscape. From his early railways such as the Hetton Colliery line and the Stockton & Darlington Railway, to the greatly influential Liverpool & Manchester Railway,

George pursued his dream with vigour and native wit. He made mistakes, of course, but who has not?

Did the efforts of George Stephenson and lieutenants such as Robert, and Joseph Locke, result in an avoidance of work? Before the railways it took the fastest stage coaches some 37 hours to get from Newcastle to London, with numerous horse changes along the way. In June 1844, a railway train reached Gateshead from London in just under $9\frac{1}{2}$ hours. Never before in the history of the world had anyone covered 303 miles in so short a time, nor saved so much work in doing so.

Stafford M. Linsley

Joseph Swan – electrical illuminator

New inventions were the excitement of the Victorian age, and the Sunderland born Joseph Swan (1828-1914) was one of many children who raided the local library to study them. Inquisitive and restless, he was apprenticed to a Sunderland druggist at 13, but when the partners died he transferred to John Mawson, at Mosley Street, Newcastle. Mawson encouraged him, building a small laboratory above the shop, and in the 1840s, Swan began experimenting with lighting.

The 'carbon filament incandescent lamp' that he patented in the 1860s beat Edison by twenty years, but contemporary vacuum pumps could not remove enough air from the lamps and soot and gasses soon built up. In the late 1870s, with new and better pumps, he returned to his experiments, demonstrating his lamp to the Newcastle Chemical Society. Next he followed Edison (who patented his own light bulb in 1879) in using a high resistance filament, which needed less current, and then set up the Swan Electric Light Company, defusing a threatened row with his American rival by merging in the Edison & Swan United Company in 1882. The two inventors worked well together. In 1880, Swan wrote generously to Edison 'I had the mortification one fine morning of finding you on my trace and in several particulars ahead of me – but now I think I have shot ahead of you'. But much remained to do and there was room for both of them 'in carrying out this gigantic work'.

Swan's other great inventions were in photography, including the production of collodion, the first method for carbon-printing, dry plate processing and bromide paper. He was a tireless worker, shouldering burdens with no apparent strain. His partner Mawson, died in a tragic accident in 1867. That year Swan's wife Frances also died, leaving him with three small children: four years later he married her sister Hannah, and had five more children. As well as his inventions, he took on a bookselling business, sold scientific equipment, lectured and set up an art gallery. He lived at Low Fell, Gateshead, but since his company was based in London, in 1883 he moved south. A jovial character, with long hair and snowy beard, he received the *Legion d'Honneur* in Paris in 1881 – when the city was lit with electric light – was elected to the Royal Society, became President of the Institute of Electrical Engineers, and was knighted in 1904. He died in 1914, just before he was due to receive the freedom of the City of Newcastle.

Jenny Uglow

Scholars

Tyneside may be many miles from the dreaming spires and ivory towers of Oxford and Cambridge, but the region has produced and nurtured many fine scholars whose work has changed the way people think.

The Venerable Bede

In the 8th century Tyneside was at the centre of European culture because it was home to the Venerable Bede, arguably the greatest scholar in the Western world at that time.

Bede, born in 673, spent his life from the age of seven at the twin monasteries of Wearmouth-Jarrow. He is called 'the Father of English

History' because of his great work, *The Ecclesiastical History of the English People*, covering 800 years and spanning five volumes. He finished it in 731. He also wrote more than 70 other books, covering topics like theology, science, poetry, astronomy, and mathematics.

A page from Bede's book on the reckoning of time includes instructions for counting from zero to 9,999 on ten fingers. In this work Bede also explained the calculation for working out the dates of Easter and argued that the moon dragged the tides around the Earth.

The scriptorium at Jarrow, where books were copied by hand, could not keep up with the demand for Bede's works from across Europe.

Bede died on 25 May, 735, aged 63 and by the 11th century a cult had developed at Jarrow at what was identified as Bede's tomb.

1,300 years later, his writings are still being published and consulted. His writings played a key role in European learning and it is said that his impact on contemporary thought was as profound at that of Charles Darwin in the 19th century.

Bede's tomb is now in Durham Cathedral. Today the great scholar is remembered at Bede's World in Jarrow, with its museum and 11-acre Anglo-Saxon farm. Nearby is St Paul's Church, whose dedication stone is dated April 23, 685 – the earliest surviving in any English church. This was the community that produced the Codex Amiatinus, the oldest surviving Bible in the world. It is one of three originally created at the monastery and its 2,060 pages used the skins of 515 animals.

Tony Henderson

The Reverend Henry Bourne – local historian

Although not the earliest known historian of Newcastle (that was William Grey who gave us his *Chorographia* in the 17th century) Henry Bourne painstakingly researched his native town and produced lasting historical works of reference, including his *History of Newcastle upon Tyne*.

Henry Bourne was the son of a tailor. He was born in Newcastle in 1694 and was apprenticed in 1709 to Barnabas Watson, a glazier based in the Side. Bourne does not seem to have enjoyed the work and returned to full-time education at the Queen Elizabeth Grammar school. With the help of 'kind friends' he was able to attend Christ's College, Cambridge and attained a BA in 1720 and an MA in 1724. Later that year he was appointed curate of All Hallows (now All Saints) in Newcastle and remained there until his death. Bourne's heavy workload at All Hallows included conducting morning and evening prayers seven days a week as well as baptisms, marriages, funerals, visiting the sick, relieving the poor and giving spiritual advice. All Hallows was reported as being 'one of the largest cures (parishes) in the Kingdom' and Bourne was said to be 'universally loved' for his devotion to the work.

Bourne published a number religious works, but his reputation rests on his research and documentation of local history, which was remarkable considering his heavy workload in the parish. In 1725 Bourne published *Antiquities of the Common People*, which gave an account of local customs and identified those which he thought should be retained and encouraged.

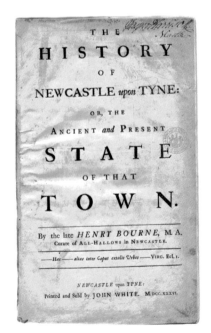

His principal historical work was *The History of Newcastle upon Tyne, or the Ancient and Present State of that Town*. There have been many testaments to Bourne's historical work, but possibly the greatest (and probably unintended) compliment was from Brand, who published a comprehensive history of Newcastle in 1789 and quoted Bourne on nearly every page.

Bourne lived in Silver Street next to All Hallows and died in 1733 after a lingering illness.

Jack and John Leslie

Charles Hutton was born in Newcastle on 14 August 1737. Like his father he first worked as a pitman, but as a result of an injury he was unable to continue this work. He attended several schools in Newcastle and later became a schoolmaster in Jesmond, subsequently moving his school into Newcastle. In 1760 he married a distant relative, Isabella Hutton, and they had a son and three daughters.

Hutton published tracts on arithmetic and mensuration (the latter illustrated by Thomas Bewick). In 1770, at the invitation of the Corporation of Newcastle, he produced a plan of the town. In 1772 he published *The Principles of Bridges*, a book written as a result of the destruction of the Tyne Bridge in a flood the previous year; it covered all aspects of bridge design and construction.

In 1773, Hutton left Newcastle, his wife and family to become Professor of Mathematics at the Royal Military Academy, Woolwich. There he taught and wrote; it was said that 'his skill and patience as an instructor were generally acknowledged' and that he was 'the most popular of English mathematical writers ... at once concise and perspicuous'.

For ten years from 1774 he was a Fellow of the Royal Society. He contributed significant papers and in 1779 was awarded a LLD degree by Edinburgh University. Throughout his stay at the Academy he wrote books and tracts on mathematical topics.

He never returned to Newcastle although at the time of his death he was planning a visit by steamship from the Thames. He maintained an interest in Newcastle, contributing to the Royal Jubilee School, the Schoolmasters' Association and the Literary and Philosophical Society. He died on 27 January 1823 and was buried at Charlton, Kent.

Robert W. Rennison

Artists, Artistes and works of art

Tyneside has long been famous for its industry and the ingenuity of its people, but it also has a rich cultural heritage.

Charles Avison – musician

Newcastle's famed nightlife is the modern, somewhat underdressed, equivalent of the posh assemblies that followed Charles Avison's fortnightly subscription concerts of music held in the Groat Market Assembly Rooms in the mid-18th century. They were the unmissable peaks of Newcastle's social calendar, with dancing, card-playing, showing off the new dress, wig or waistcoat – and the all important gossip. They ensured a full house for the concert preliminary, with local boy Avison shrewdly letting in ladies at half price and discouraging bustles (hooped skirts) to allow more room.

A Newcastle Wait's son (the Waits were the town band), born in 1709, close to where The Gate now dominates Newgate Street, Avison was off to London in his teens to learn his trade as a fiddle player from the Italian master Geminiani. There he eyed the fashionable craze for music concerts at a hundred or so venues, spearheaded by the Saxon import Handel's music. London's booming economy was sucking in Europe's best musicians, rather as today's Premiership TV money lures the world's top footballers.

Avison must have thought 'I'll take that back to the Tyne'. The coaly Tyne. For Newcastle was a burgeoning Klondike. Its virtual monopoly of the only movable energy source in Europe, as the World's first Industrial Revolution gathered pace, was creating the equivalent of today's oil sheiks. All that wealth, all those entrepreneurs, factory owners and engineers: all ambitious, intelligent – and culture hungry. Avison perhaps dreamt of his concerts in his Newcastle: concerts a sedan chair ride away, not a five day coach ordeal to London.

Charles Avison, 1761.

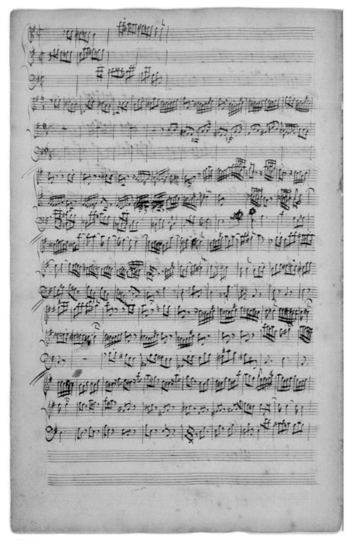

So back in Newcastle and needing an income, he launched his concerts that ran from 1735 to out-live him by 50 years. He supplemented his stipends as organist at St John's and St Nicholas' churches by teaching the gentry and their children, who then formed the backbone of his Groat Market orchestra, with the tricky solo parts played by him-self and the occasional professional. Soon an acute country-wide short-age of new music forced him to become an almost compulsive composer to keep his own concerts alive.

Avison, single-hand-edly, made Newcastle England's greatest provin-cial music centre of the time – 250 years before The Sage Gateshead. His were the earliest provincial subscription concerts in England. His music was snapped up by societies throughout the land: oozing with melody, playable by amateurs and coming with long prefaces telling you how to play it. Avison, an 18th century Andrew Lloyd Webber, got up the noses of the London professionals, but everyone else couldn't get enough of his work.

'… the most important English concerto composer of the 18th cen-tury', says the *New Grove Dictionary of Music*. Avison wrote tuneful, accessible, easy listening music, with solo violin passages of indelible beauty that float like thistledown on the breeze, exhilarating breathtaking sections like rollercoasters, and always that unique Avison Northumbrian/Italianate hybrid sound. Recently the first complete recording of his Opus 6 – his finest – from the Newcastle-based Avison Ensemble* sold out in one week.

And he could write too. His *An Essay on Musical Expression of 1752* is the first treatise of musical criticism in English. It created a storm of disapproval and consummated his alienation from London with such comments as Vivaldi, 'only fit amusement for children' and Handel, 'to suit public taste sometimes descends to the lowest'. The Avison Archive, held at Newcastle Libraries, now boasts two of his workbooks – treasure troves of unpublished music from Avison and his contemporaries.

Avison died in 1770, just turned 61, after being caught out in a May blizzard, hopefully wearing more than today's customary Geordie-male uniform T-shirt. Now almost unknown, even in Newcastle, this unfairly neglected national composer is remembered by his gravestone and a privately endowed commemorative plaque (both at St Andrew's Church); a street in Arthur's Hill; and an increasingly known legacy of exuberant music. Music as Geordie as *The Keel Row* and *The Blaydon Races*, from a Geordie who remained loyal to his roots.

www.avisonensemble.com

❧ *David Hughes*

The Avison Ensemble.

Thomas Bewick – artist and engraver

Thomas Bewick is the king of British wood-engraving, and his art is rooted in Tyneside. He was born in August 1753 at Cherryburn, near Mickley, where his father had a smallholding and two small landsale collieries. A wayward child, at school in Ovingham he was a constant truant: he fished, swam in the burns and played 'savages' on the fells with his friends. Although he had never been taught, Bewick drew anywhere he could, on books, walls, floors. At 14 he was apprenticed to the Newcastle engraver, Ralph Beilby, and when he left home for the workshop at Amen Corner, he thought his heart 'was like to break'.

The engraving work at Beilby's, and later at Bewick's own firm, ranged from shop cards to coffin plates, a window on the life of Newcastle. In 1776, he travelled through Scotland, and then briefly worked in London. But he soon returned: 'I would rather be herding sheep on Mickley bank top,' he declared 'than remain in London although for doing so, I was to be made Premier of England'. Six years later he married Isabella Elliot, and they went on to have three daughters and a son, Robert.

His woodcuts were often finished by candle-light after work. With Beilby providing the text, in 1790 he published *A General History of Quadrupeds*, an encylopedia of animals from the tiger to the field-mouse. His great *History of British Birds* – which appeared in two volumes, *Land Birds* in 1797, and *Water Birds* in 1804, was the first field-guide for ordinary people, a turning point in natural history. As a

diversion, Bewick drew little tail-pieces (or 'tale-pieces' as he punningly called them), full of detail of country life on Tyneside. But although Romantics like Wordsworth liked to see him as a rough untutored genius, he was a shrewd businessman and also a passionate radical. A friend of Thomas Spence, he supported the

American colonists, welcomed the French revolution, damned greedy landlords, enclosures and game laws, and constantly attacked 'aristocratic' war and imperialism.

He went on to publish an illustrated *Aesop's Fables* and began *A History of British Fishes*, but this was never finished. His last vignette shows his coffin being carried from Cherryburn to the boat that would carry it across to Ovingham church. He died in 1828 and on his death-bed he was asked what he was thinking about, and replied 'that he had been devising subjects for new tail-pieces'.

Jenny Uglow

Basil Bunting – finest poet

Finest poet from the North East? There's a conundrum. Poets abound in the North East and fine ones, too. Tony Harrison makes your spine tingle while Sean O'Brien works wonders with the language. Tom Pickard, W.N. Herbert, Linda France and Gillian Allnutt are other bright stars in a constellation. Barry MacSweeney and Julia Darling made their mark before leaving us prematurely. This list is by no means comprehensive. But it doesn't take too much pondering before Basil Bunting comes to the fore.

Born in Scotswood on 1 March 1900, Bunting was a Northumbrian born and bred. An essay published to accompany an exhibition at

Northumbrian poet Basil Bunting pictured beside the river Rawthey, Cumbria, 1980.

Durham University Library – home of the Basil Bunting Poetry Archive – in 1987 begins: 'Basil Bunting is the most important poet in the North East of England since Caedmon in the late 7th Century.'

If that weren't enough to clinch it, there's the biography by Richard Caddel and Anthony Flowers, *Basil Bunting: A Northern Life*, published in 1997. It explains how the young Tom Pickard, in the early 1960s, encouraged the old man to take up poetry again after a long hiatus. Subsequently he wrote his masterpiece, *Briggflatts*, and became a star performer at the Morden Tower poetry venue established in Newcastle by Tom and wife Connie.

Basil Bunting led a fascinating life. Born a Quaker, he was imprisoned as a conscientious objector in the First World War. He went to London in 1919, met some of the leading literary lights and subsequently moved to Paris. In the 1920s he worked for Ford Madox Ford and met Ezra Pound, Ernest Hemingway, T.S. Eliot and D.H. Lawrence. In 1937 he studied at a nautical college in Newcastle and then skippered a millionaire's schooner. He enlisted in the RAF during the Second World War when he had his first experience of Persia (now Iran). After the war he worked there as intelligence officer and journalist.

But in *Briggflatts*, published in 1965, his northern roots were exposed. In a note, he described the epic poem as 'an autobiography, but not a record of fact'. The Durham essay lauds the 'compression and economy of statement' in his work, further praising his powers of acute observation and grasp of the significant. Similarity is drawn with Wordsworth and comparisons made with Eliot and Pound. That's not bad company to be in.

As Tom Pickard noted after his death in 1985: 'It was because of Basil that we were able to attract all the best poets to Newcastle.'

They are still coming.

David Whetstone

The Mayor's Barge on the Tyne, c.1826-30, J.W. Carmichael (1799-1868)

Looking at Newcastle today from Carmichael's viewpoint on the Gateshead shore – below the Sage – it is easy to forget that Newcastle grew to importance not so much as a town but as a port. Hence the two themes that underpin this iconic panorama: the hegemony of the city over the river Tyne, and the never-ending streams of maritime commerce that fed its wealth. Cunningly, the artist creates a calm circlet of water and light that, despite a busy foreground and alluring 'distant prospect', draws the eye into the middle distance with its golden subject – the Mayoral Barge. This was no grubby trading 'barge'. But, aping its peers, the Lord Mayor's and State Barges of the 'London River', it was an ornate processional carriage afloat: the vehicle in which Newcastle's mayor annually asserted the city's authority over the navigable Tyne.

Having duly acknowledged his powerful patrons, the Mayor and corporation, the artist then revels in depicting the Tyne's many layers of maritime activity. These same activities had occupied his pre-painterly life, serving aboard ships and ashore in Farrington's shipyard. To the left, an unmistakable Yorkshire 'billyboy', the *Ann of Hull*, lies in the stream, her sails drying (to prevent rot) and crew busily occupied on deck, whilst a Tyne wherry lies close alongside to attend her loading. Likely, the *Ann* is a 'constant trader', plying regularly twixt Humber and Tyne. To this coaster's right, and more prestigious by far, is a substantial deep sea merchantman receiving a new, three-ton spar

*The Mayor's Barge on the Tyne, c. 1826-30, by J.W. Carmichael, Laing Art Gallery
(Tyne & Wear Museums).*

from a commonplace Tyne keel; testament to what brawn, 'takles' (pulley blocks), and seamanlike skill could, and did, do. About to be received too – at the ship's rough boarding ladder – is a red-gowned and bonneted lady: an intending passenger, or the captain's wife, who now can tell? Beyond, in distant prospect, and artistically disposed to leave a clear view of the city's imposing Guildhall and its pillared extension (the fishmarket), several more such vessels line the quayside. No common colliers these, but high class carriers, familiar with the Indies (East or West) and Britain's ocean flung colonies.

What then of the Coal Trade and the Tyne's famous collier brigs? Downriver, out of sight, at the river's staith-lined middle reaches, or topping up their cargoes from tide-borne keels in Shields salty harbour. Tactfully, Carmichael barely hints at this carboniferous heart of darkness: a coal-laden, ebb-borne keel 'keps' its mast to slide under the low-arched bridge, whilst another, mast and sail raised again, passes downriver out of scene. And, above all, countless smoky streamers issue from the townscape chimneys, markers of coal-fuelled prosperity. The wind is westerly, and all seems set fair.

Enough of such a description, though there is much, much more – Who, in all conscience, could argue this is not Tyneside's finest maritime painting?

Adrian Osler

Dame Catherine Cookson – finest romantic novelist

South Shields-born author Catherine Cookson was one of Britain's most widely read novelists. She was born Kate McMullen on June 27 1906, at Leam Lane, Tyne Dock, South Shields. The illegitimate child of an alcoholic mother, Kate Fawcett, she was raised by her grandmother Rose McMullen and her step-grandfather John McMullen. She thought that her unmarried mother was her sister. Her books reflected her deprived childhood and many of her stories were set in the region. She later moved to East Jarrow, which became the setting for one of her best-known novels, *The Fifteen Streets*.

She went on to write almost 100 books, selling more than 123 million copies, with her works being translated into at least 20 languages. She also wrote under the pseudonym Catherine Marchant and a name

One of the most popular authors in the library – some of Newcastle City Library's lending stock

derived from her birth name, Katie Mullen.

She left school at 13 and, after working in domestic service, took a job in the laundry at the workhouse in Harton Lane, South Shields. In 1929 she moved south to run the laundry at the the workhouse in Hastings in Sussex where she bought a large Victorian House and took in lodgers to boost her income.

In 1940, aged 34, she married Tom Cookson, a teacher at Hastings Grammar School. Sadly the couple did not have any children. Catherine suffered four miscarriages and was diagnosed as suffering from a rare vascular disease, telangiectasia.

She began writing as a form of therapy to tackle her depression, and joined the Hastings Writer's Group. Her first novel, *Kate Hannigan*, was published in 1950 and labelled a romance, which displeased her as her books, she said, were historical novels about the people and conditions she knew.

Many of her books were transferred to stage, film and radio, making her a multi-millionaire. It was on television, however that she achieved her greatest success, with a series of dramas on ITV lasting over a decade and achieving huge ratings. She also indulged in discreet philanthropy, supporting many causes in the North East as well as medical research – she gave more than £1m for research into a cure for the illness that had afflicted her.

In later life, Catherine and Tom returned to the North East and settled down in Corbridge in the Tyne Valley and later in Langley, a small village nearby. But as her health declined, they moved to Newcastle to be nearer medical facilities.

She received the freedom of South Tyneside, today known as Catherine Cookson Country, and an honorary degree from the University of Newcastle. There were other honours too. She was named Writer of the Year by the Variety Club of Great Britain and voted personality of the North East. In 1985 she received the order of the British Empire and was made a Dame in 1993. She died aged 91, just 16 days before her 92nd birthday on 11 June 1998 at her home in Newcastle. Her husband, Tom, died shortly afterwards on 28 June, also in Newcastle; he was 86.

Ian Wilson

Jimmy Forsyth – Scotswood's finest photographer

Jimmy Forsyth, well-known amateur photographer of the Scotswood area of Newcastle, was actually born in Barry, South Wales, in 1913. Barry was an industrial, port town, but as a young man Jimmy found it difficult to get work in the depression of the 1930s and joined the merchant navy. This took him away from Wales for several years and perhaps gave him the curiosity and wanderlust that eventually brought him to Tyneside in the 1940s.

Famously, Jimmy worked at his job as a fitter in Prudhoe for just four days before an accident with a lathe left him blind in one eye, and although he continued to work at ICI for a while, the return of employees from the forces left him once more unemployed. It was around this time, at the same time as looking for work, that Jimmy started to take photographs of his surroundings, and of people he knew in Scotswood, where he was living.

Prints of Jimmy's work from this period are preserved

Jimmy recorded the demolition of Scotswood. Here is Sycamore Street, 1961.

at Tyne & Wear Archives Service in distinctive tartan-covered albums. With their hand-written captions they record Jimmy's interest in the changing scene around him and the longer history of Newcastle, as well as dramatic events such as the sinking of the *Cyprian Coast* in the Tyne, the return of the victorious Newcastle United from the 1955 FA Cup Final, fires and motor accidents.

The early photographs show characteristics of Jimmy's work that can be seen throughout. First the systematic recording of scenes of demolition or building work, sometimes over many months. The monochrome shots of 60s Scotswood are paralleled by the 1980s colour

The Quayside, St George's Day, 1958.
The boy with the pigeon, right, was photographed in 1956.

views of the building of the new Redheugh Bridge or new supermarkets and shopping malls. Favourite haunts such as the Grainger Market are chronicled over decades so that the changes in stalls and stallholders can be traced precisely.

Portraits of adults and children posed on street corners or in the town are also favourites, with teddy boys giving way to punks as the years go by. Many of the people in the pictures are known to Jimmy – his friends and neighbours – but others are snatched pictures of workmen or buskers who may only know him by reputation, if at all. There

is hardly a photograph, however, where the subject looks unhappy at being snapped. Jimmy seems always to have been able to strike up a rapport that has frequently resulted in a striking image.

From the many thousands of Jimmy's pictures at Tyne & Wear Archives it is difficult to pick a 'finest' but one that captures its time is the portrait of the young boy in his new cowboy outfit taken in Scotswood on 2 January 1958. The outfit is obviously a Christmas present, but the boy stands on his own in the middle of the snowy street, with only Jimmy and his camera to witness his finery and capture the moment for posterity.

᳁ *Liz Rees*

Jimmy Forsyth

Jimmy managed to get himself into some risky and dramatic places by talking people into letting him have access, as in this shot of the dismantling of the old Scotswood Bridge in 1967.

John Gilroy, illustrator

John Gilroy was a superb illustrator and artist who is probably best remembered for his work for the brewer Guinness.

His best-known works include the posters featuring the girder carrier and the woodcutter from the *Guinness For Strength* campaigns of the 1930s. He is also famous for the Guinness animals, including the lion, toucan, gnu and kangaroo with their long-suffering zoo-keeper, who appeared on advertisements, posters and waiters' trays from the 1930s to the 1960s.

John Gilroy was born on 30 May 1898 in Whitley Bay, one of a family of five boys and three girls. His father, William, was a draughtsman and marine landscape painter who quickly realised that his son was going to follow in his footsteps.

Young John started by copying cartoons from magazines like *Punch*. By the age of 15 he commissioned by *Evening Chronicle* to produce cartoons of entertainers playing at theatres in Newcastle.

John won an art scholarship to Armstrong College Art School, part of Durham University, but his studies were interrupted by the First World War. He served with the Royal Artillery in France and the Middle East. Afterwards he moved to the Royal College of Art in London, graduating in 1923, and staying on for a further two years as a teacher.

In 1925 he began working for Benson's advertising agency on campaigns for Virol and Skipper sardines followed by Macleans, Monk & Glass Custard and Bovril. From 1926 to 1933, with fellow artist William Brearley he brought to life eccentric characters like Signor Spaghetti and Baron de Beef which were seen on advertising hoardings across the UK.

But it was Benson's contract with Guinness that was to make Gilroy's name and he continued to produce advertisements for them until the 1960s even though he had left Benson's years before.

In 1975 Gilroy was awarded an honorary MA by Newcastle University and in 1981 he was appointed a Freeman of the City of London. He died at Guildford on 11 April 1985 at the age of 86 and is buried at Ampney St Peter in Gloucestershire near the home of his son and family.

Ian Wilson

James Hill – virtuoso fiddler

Nineteenth century virtuoso fiddler, James Hill, left behind around 50 tunes, some of which have found their way into recordings of everything from American Bluegrass to Irish and Scots music.

In the 1840s, with all kinds of heavy industry booming on Tyneside, countryfolk as well as Scottish and Irish immigrants flooded into the towns of the North East. The pub trade was thriving. North Shields-born Hill was one of a bunch of professional pub fiddlers who were the 19th century equivalent of the juke box. Customers made their requests, put down their money, and enjoyed a drink while they listened.

Hill also played at dances, public functions and race meetings. He wrote his own music. Many of his works commemorate great race-horses of the day, like *Beeswing*, *Underhand*, *The Flying Dutchman*, and *XYZ*. Others celebrate pubs such as the Pear Tree, Locomotive and Free Trade as well as the Hawk on Bottle Bank in Gateshead where Hill is believed to been the landlord.

The Free Trade pub, celebrated by James Hill, photographed in 1913. It is still a great pace to hear local music.

Other tunes are named after events and characters such as industrialist Sir Charles Attwood and Earl Grey. One beguiling work is called *The Lads Like Beer*.

Hill's tunes have spread around the English-speaking world and his best-known composition, the *High Level Hornpipe*, written for the opening of the High Level Bridge in 1849, is used as a test piece in fiddle competitions from Texas to Seattle and from Shetland to the west of Ireland. Richard Thornton, himself a fiddler and founder of the Moss Empire Theatre organisation, wrote of being taken by his father to hear various fiddle players.

'Our first port of call was to hear Jimmy Hill. Jimmy wrote several very fine hornpipes and many more and he was the daddy of them all at hornpipe playing.' Contemporary accounts say that James Hill had 'was unapproachable for power, vivacity and correct intonation.'

Hill's music has been revived by modern day fiddlers like Tom McConville (who grew up as part of a musical family on Newcastle's Scotswood Road and has recorded an entire CD of Hill's music called *Fiddler's Fancy*) and Northumbrian pipers such as Pauline Cato.

Hill is believed to have died from TB in his 40s, but he embodied the popular Tyneside culture of his day and his musical legacy lives on.

Tony Henderson

Alan Hull – Tyneside's finest singer-songwriter

Alan Hull was perhaps best known as a singer, songwriter and front man in Lindisfarne, one of the most successful bands to come out of the North East.

Alan was born in 1945 and his musical career took off in the 1960s as a singer/song writing member of the Chosen Few, a local band for whom he composed a number of published tracks. He left the band to become a psychiatric nurse and part-time folk singer. Alan has said that during his time as a psychiatric nurse he met some of the most inspiring people in his life. In the late 1960s Alan, who was heavily involved in the North East folk scene, joined forces with Brethren whose name changed to Lindisfarne in 1970. Alan made his name through his beautifully crafted songs including *Lady Eleanor* and the anthem *Fog on the Tyne*. Lindisfarne achieved both critical and commercial success with their first two albums.

Alan's debut solo album, *Pipedream*, was recorded in 1973 and in part inspired by his work in the psychiatric hospital. Although Alan remained with Lindisfarne throughout the 70s and 80s, he continued his solo career with albums including Squire. He was still very active in the 1990s performing his back catalogue to a loyal following throughout the UK.

Alan was also a committed Socialist who also spent some time in local politics.

His life was tragically cut short in 1995 when he died of a heart attack, but his songs are still part of Tyneside culture. From the poignant *Winter Song* to the strident *Marshall Riley's Army*, Alan's songs have featured in annual tributes by fellow musicians in the North East.

It has been said that 'Hull never wasted a lyric, every line was meant to count, and even if we sometimes failed to understand, his intention was always honest and true, dark and humorous'.

Jack and John Leslie, with thanks to Ray Laidlaw

Lindisfarne, one of Tyneside's favourite bands.

The Blaydon Races – a study from life, 1903 by William Irving (1866-1943)

Not many artists have painted a picture and woken up the next day to find themselves just as famous as the people in it. Until that exciting day in 1903 when William Irving's *Blaydon Races* went on show in the window of a Newcastle art dealer he had been a little known illustrator for the local newspapers. By the time the paint had dried he had become almost as well known as any of the 26 characters painted into his sprawling composition – Nanny the Mazer, of Scotswood, Puncher Anderson of Gallowgate, and Strolling Mike of Gateshead, to name but a few.

The race meeting at Blaydon, long celebrated in Geordie Ridley's rollicking tune, was a natural for Irving's skill as an illustrator. Certainly the Newcastle public thought so on the day the painting first

A detail from William Irving's Blaydon Races, 1903, a favourite Tyneside painting. Shipley Art Gallery (Tyne & Wear Museums).

went on show. The police had to ask the gallery manager to close the blinds as the crowds were stopping the traffic!

Its fame has continued to the present time, thanks to its endless reproduction in prints and on table mats and menus, not to mention its exhibition over the next century in two of the city's most famous hotels – first the County, and then the Gosforth Park. But this icon of Geordie pride almost left the region for ever in November 2002 when it was sent to London for sale.

Only then, perhaps, did it dawn on everyone that the North East public held the painting in such affectionate regard and £110,000 was found by Tyne & Wear Museums to buy it. It now hangs in the Shipley Art Gallery, Gateshead, in the same borough as Blaydon where those famous Tyneside races were held. 'Oh! Lads ye shud a' seen us gannin'.

Marshall Hall

Dame Flora Robson, actor and movie star

In the 1920s and 30s many young women dreamed of going to Hollywood, to star opposite the world's leading film actors. One of the few to turn their fantasy into reality was Flora Robson. Born in South Shields on 28 March 1902, the daughter of a marine surveyor, she became a successful stage and screen actress and, in 1939, was invited to Hollywood by Samuel Goldwyn to join the cast of his production of *Wuthering Heights*. Over the next four years she appeared in several Hollywood films, playing opposite Gary Cooper, Errol Flynn, William Holden, Paul Muni, George Raft and Laurence Olivier. In 1946 she was nominated for an Academy Award as Best Actress in a Supporting Role for her performance as Angelique, a mulatto servant, in the film *Saratoga Trunk*. She was narrowly beaten by Anne Baxter who took the Oscar for her role in *The Razor's Edge*.

Flora Robson made her way to the top by acting ability rather than good looks. She once said that the words 'She was a plain woman' would be inscribed on her tombstone, and added that she would have traded some of her acting talent for a bit of beauty. 'I lost out on a great many parts by not being pretty. I wanted to play Juliet, but was cast as the nurse'.

Did Flora Robson achieve 'star' status? Well, David Shipman

Dame Flora Robson, 1934.

includes her in his book *The Great Movie Stars – The Golden Years* (Angus and Robertson, 1979). There she is sandwiched between the entries on Edward G. Robinson and Ginger Rogers. Dame Flora acted in over 50 films and enjoyed a distinguished stage career, in which she appeared in 113 plays, including many London West End and Broadway productions. Over the years she received several acting awards and honorary degrees, and in 1960 was made a Dame of the British Empire for her services to the theatre. There is a Dame Flora Robson Avenue on the Simonside Estate on South Tyneside, and the Jesmond Playhouse was renamed the Flora Robson Playhouse in her honour, not least because she played a major part in getting it reopened in 1960. Unfortunately it was demolished ten years later to make way for a motorway that was never built.

Dame Flora Robson made her last stage appearance at the age of 70 but continued to accept parts in films, radio and television for several years. She spent her retirement in Brighton and died at the Royal Sussex Hospital on 7 July 1984. Several obituaries described her as one of Britain's finest actresses – and few people would disagree.

Archie Potts

Sol Sheckman – Tyneside's cinema tycoon

These days, mainstream cinemas are owned by multinational companies controlled by accountants and the films we see have, for the most part, substituted computer generated effects for the old tradition of storytelling. Fifty years ago cinemas had character and individuality and the people who ran them stood or fell by their own efforts.

The best known of the cinema tycoons was J. Arthur Rank, then owner of the Gaumont and Odeon cinema circuits. His Tyneside equivalent, Sol Sheckman, is now almost forgotten and his creation, Essoldo cinemas, is long gone.

Sol Sheckman was born on 10 September 1891 at Plock in Russian Poland. He was the eldest of three brothers and two sisters who emigrated to South Shields in 1902 with their parents. Moving a year later to North Shields, the family established itself as dealers in sailors' clothing and quickly prospered. Sol married Ester Cohen at Newcastle Synagogue in 1914. The family flourished as clothes dealers until 1924, at which time Sol entered the cinema business.

How precisely he did this has not been discovered, but it is plausible that he was involved with a group of South Shields men who established a company called Northern Victory Theatres. Certainly, two of the first cinemas he owned, the Victory at Crawcrook and the Palace, High Spen, had been part of the company's portfolio. He soon built up a circuit of small cinemas in County Durham, notably in Crook, where by 1927 he owned all three of the town's picture palaces.

In the early 1900s, Sol expanded his interests in Blyth and in 1938 built his first new cinema, the Blyth Essoldo (the name created by combining elements of family forenames, ESther, SOLomon, and DOrothy (their daughter)). His flagship cinema, the Newcastle Essoldo in Westgate Road, was opened in August 1938. The building of these two new cinemas seemed to suggest that Sol was intent on following the example of his contemporary, Oscar Deutsch, creator of the Odeon chain, but World War II intervened.

Sol Sheckman in the 1920s.

At the end of the war, Sol Sheckman owned 12 cinemas, all in the North East, but this was soon to change. Prevented from erecting new cinemas by the post-war restriction on luxury building, Sol set off on a new course, which was to last for the next 14 years, of buying or leasing any cinema which came on to the market, until in 1959 he had 196 of them across England. In addition to his Newcastle office, initially in Bath Lane, then in Westgate Road (at the heart of Newcastle's film trade), he had opened offices in London, where he was represented by his younger brother Mark.

Sol was one of the earliest supporters of the CinemaScope process, which he installed – along with four-track magnetic

Queues for the Al Jolson Story at Newcastle's Essoldo, October 1948.

sound – in the majority of his cinemas. An alliance with Twentieth Century Fox brought a host of popular films in this format to Essoldo cinemas.

Sol was that unusual combination of ruthless businessman and shy personality, who normally kept well away from the limelight: not for him the glamorous film premieres in the company of the stars of the day. He spent most of his time doing deals for cinemas to add to his chain, which was strongest on Merseyside, Portsmouth, the Midlands, and of course the North East. At the end his cinema portfolio was reckoned to be worth £12m.

Sol Sheckman died aged 72 on 5 August 1963. His family continued with the business for almost a decade, but in a climate of declining revenues from cinemas and changing public tastes, sold their remaining 52 operating cinemas to Classic for £4.3m in 1972 and their 36 bingo clubs to Ladbroke's for £9.1m in 1973. And so the name Essoldo vanished from the land.

❧ *Frank Manders*

Benjamin Ferdinand Simpson – exuberant architect

If Glasgow can have its Charles Rennie Mackintosh, then maybe Newcastle can have its Benjamin Ferdinand Simpson? 'Benjamin who?' I hear you ask.

Well, you might not know his name but you will certainly know his buildings. Does Emerson Chambers ring a bell, that wildly exuberant building near Grey's Monument that was Dillon's and is now Waterstone's bookshop? Or what about Half Moon Chambers, that jolly pub building in the Bigg Market with huge witches' hats on the roof? Now you remember!

Well, Simpson and his architectural partners designed them both.

Simpson was a local lad who began his architectural training with John E. Watson in Newcastle in 1874. He joined the firm as an architect in 1886 and from then until the end of his career in 1914, he worked on his own and in productive partnerships.

Simpson's Emerson Chambers, a fairytale building of curliques and turrets. It pays to keep looking up in the city, there are many architectural treasures to be found.

Anna Flowers

The personal style he developed over the years, is a curious and fascinating mixture of personalised Art Nouveau, Baroque revival and Eastern exotic – a truly innovative and eclectic architecture, with a touch of Northern (Geordie?) humour – all made possible by the wealth and confidence of his local clients. Emerson Chambers is all the things we dream a building should be – charming, witty and inventive. It is not a building to describe, but one to just enjoy and wonder at.

Anna Flowers

Half Moon Chambers.

Half Moon Inn, Bigg Market c.1910.

The stone fantasy that is Half Moon Chambers is also covered in memorable detail: beautifully carved names over the doors, intricate black iron balconies with white half moon motifs woven into the fancy metalwork, wonderfully carved columns and pilasters, fancy stone sills and window heads, all topped out with a curly central gable and jolly witches' hat dormers – dominating the Bigg Market in the most delightful way possible.

Simpson's list of local successes also includes the grandly beautiful and practical Tramways Depot on Melbourne Street, the delicate and sober corner building of 1 Mosley Street, the clever shop front at 50 Dean Street and (possibly) the fabulous Reid's shop front in Blackett Street, the most memorable shop front in the City Centre.

For all their cleverness and skill, their attention to detail and to quality materials, the one outstanding principle that Simpson's buildings demonstrate is how much fun architecture can become in the right hands. What a contrast to the sober elegance of Richard Grainger's work – but the richness of contrast is just what makes the historic heart of Newcastle the splendid place it is. Thank you old Mr Grainger, and a special thank you to the ever youthful Mr Simpson too!

❧ *David Lovie*

C.P. Taylor – Tyneside's finest playwright

North of the border, apparently, they used to call C.P. Taylor 'Scotland's greatest living playwright'. But he lived and worked in Northumberland for the last 20 years of his life, writing plays for the theatre and television.

One of his most popular plays, recently revived by Live Theatre, was *And a Nightingale Sang*, as affectionate and authentic a portrayal of wartime Tyneside as you would expect from the most dedicated Geordie.

By the time of his premature death in 1981, the North East had long embraced this passionate, talented and probably awkward man as one of its own. *And a Nightingale Sang* was the work of a man able to find laughter among tears and to recognise the quiet tragedy at the heart of apparent contentment. The play sang like the bird, brilliantly and full of life. Taylor, who never thanked his parents for calling him Cecil and brushed aside jibes that the initials really stood for Communist Party (he was a lifelong socialist and an atheist too), died the year before I moved to Newcastle and in the same year that *Good* was performed by the Royal Shakespeare Company. It was the first of his plays I ever saw and it made a deep impression.

Set in Germany after the Nazi takeover, it shows how basically decent people were swept up by a movement now regarded as evil. The

Keith Pattison / Live Theatre

And a Nightingale Sang, performed at Newcastle's Live Theatre, 2006.

question had been asked many times: How could they have allowed this to happen? Here's how. And the most chilling message you will take away from this play is just how easily it could happen to you. Real evil moves insidiously, poisoning from the inside out.

This Taylor understood, as he understood many things. In plays such as *Operation Elvis, Bandits* and *The Black And White Minstrels*, he demonstrated his shrewdness, his compassion and his uncompromising brilliance as a writer.

Over 30 years, Taylor wrote more than 70 plays. Not bad for a man born in 1929 in a rough area of Glasgow, and who left school at 14 to become a radio mechanic. He wrote for television and for the most prestigious theatre companies. He wrote for adults, teenagers and children, notably as writer in residence for the Northumberland Experimental Youth Theatre (now there's a name to conjure with).

Probably he could have made a fortune. Instead he earned lasting respect and a lot of friends in the North East and beyond.

David Whetstone

Joe Wilson – songwriter

Born in 1841, Joe Wilson is described as Tyneside's most popular bard in Allan's *Tyneside Songs*. Joe says of his family: 'me fether wes a cabinet myeker an' me muther a straw bonnet myeker, both natives of the canny auld toon'. He was born at the end of Stowell Street and he describes his own birth thus: 'twenty minutes after me forst ippeerence, te the astonishment o' neybors, Wor Tom showed his fyece, te dispute wi me whe shud be the family pet!'

At 14 Joe went to work as a printer and by 17 his first book was published. He openly stated that his aim was to have a place in the hearts of Tyneside people by writing 'bits o' hyemly sangs a think they'll sing'. While in his twenties he brought out his 'forst number of Tyneside Sangs'. Soon Joe's songs were well known. They included *The Row upon the Stairs, The Gallowgate Lad, Dinnit Clash The Door, Geordie Haud the Bairn* and of course, *Keep yor feet still Geordie Hinny*.

Joe says: 'me forst perfessional engagement wes at Pelton, December 1864, me second at the Oxford Music Hall and me thord at

WE'LL SEUN HEH WARK TE DE !

OR, THE STRIKE O' '71.

WRITTEN BY

JOE WILSON,

And sung by him at the "Oxford" Music Hall, Newcastle,
received nightly with most tremendous applause.

TEUN—"NOWT TE DE."

"On Strike !" aw hear them awful words
    Repeated i' the street,
"On strike ! ne wark !" aw hear agyen,
    Frae hundreds that aw meet,
"Three lang munths gyen,—not sattled yit !
    Wor hard-up as can be,
It cannet last, thor'll be a change,
    We'll seun heh wark te de !"

KORUS.

Walkin roond the Market,
    An' walkin doon the Kee,
The only cheerin words aw hear's
    "We'll seun heh wark te de !"

Aw see the poor cheps oot on strike
    Gan slawly throo the street,
Tho' anxshus for the latest news,
    Frev iv'ry one they meet,
They keep up one-anuther's hearts,
    As honest men shud be,
Wi' hopes the day's not distant when
    They'll all heh wark te de !

"Mair forriners !" aw hear them say
    Then one 'ill shake his heed—
"They may get plenty men as cheap,
    But is't them that they need ?
No, no ! it's real mechanicks that
    A maister likes te see,
Nine oors te him's a better thing,
    Gud men his wark te de !"

"At hyem thor's nowt but misery,
    Where happy days we've seen,
When plenty wark an' plenty keep
    Myed a' things luck soreen,
We'll heh them gud things back agyen,
    Seun settled we shall be,
Then forrin culls may tyek thor hook
    Frae wark they cannet de !"

"We'll seun heh wark te de, me lads !
    God bliss us a' we will,
Tyneside 'ill yit victorious shine,
    Wi' men o' worth an' skill,
An' happier days 'ill myek the past
    A dream o' what we see,
Men gud an' true 'ill nivor rue,
    We'll seun heh wark te de !"

All JOE WILSON'S SONG BOOKS always on hand.

CHEAP BOOKS—GREAT CHOICE ! SCHOOL BOOKS—GREAT VARIETY !

Published by THOS. ALLEN, Bookseller,

62, DEAN STREET, & 16, COLLINGWOOD STREET, NEWCASTLE.

the Tyne Concert Hall in Newcassil. Since then aw've been te nearly ivry toon in the North – wi the syem success aw've had in me native place'. Joe's professional career in effect began with a three month run at the Oxford Music Hall (not the Oxford Galleries adjacent to the Laing Art Gallery, but the establishment which has been famous for years as Balmbras, in the Cloth Market).

Joe continued to travel and perform when he was married but found it ever less agreeable to be away from home. He tried to settle back in Newcastle as landlord of the Adelaide Hotel in 1871 but after just over a year he became teetotal and started up his concert life again. When Joe was just 33 years old his health began to fail and after a long illness he died at his home in Railway Street.

He was by far the most successful Tyneside songwriter of the time and his wish to have a lasting place in the hearts of his own folk was most certainly achieved. Joe's songs went beyond those of many local songwriters by painting a comprehensive picture of Tyneside life and travelling Tynesiders carried them to all corners of the world.

The *Newcastle Weekly Chronicle* wrote a tribute to Joe after his death which included the following quotes: 'His songs have become household words in Tyneside and for many a mile round about – He made you laugh until you nearly cried – He spoke to the hearts of his readers'. His productions are merely songs and not poems. They don't pretend to be anything special but their lasting popularity has given Joe immortality.

❧ Jack and John Leslie, with acknowledgement to Pete Scott,
North East musician and songwriter

'Keep yor feet still Geordie Hinney
Let's be happy for the neet
For aa may nit be se happy thro' the day
So give us that bit comfort, keep yor feet still Geordie lad
And dinnet drive me bonny dreams away.'

A handful of oddities

These people (and a ghost) don't fit comfortably into any of our categories, but they had to be included.

William Martin – 'Philosophical Conqueror of all nations'

Who has heard of this eccentric Geordie, who propelled himself through the streets of early 19th century Newcastle on his own velocipede 'the Northumbrian eagle mail' wearing a greatcoat, a silver medal from the Royal Society pinned to his breast, and with an upturned tortoiseshell strapped to his head with brass fittings? His fellow Tynesiders should perhaps know him better than they do. Not only was he the elder brother of the quite mad Jonathan Martin, who set light to York Minster in 1829 and ended his days in Bedlam; he was also the brother of the artist and engineer John Martin, who in his day was the most famous painter in the land – friend to radicals, scientists, poets and writers alike.

Born in Tynedale in 1772, to equally eccentric parents, William spent much of his life in Wallsend, where he worked at the Howdon ropery; but he had also served for many years during the wars against France in the Northumberland militia. Here he acquired a reputation as a champion swordsman, athlete (he seems to have held a world record for the standing jump), and doggerel poet. His verses are truly awful. But he also invented things: an iron railway in an age when wagons ran on wooden rails; the spring balance; the pneumatic life-jacket; and 37 perpetual motion machines (of which the

William Martin Natural Philosopher Engraved by Him Also— 1829

Sir Isaac was a knave and a deceiver of Mankind and all kinds of People But W.M. is no such thing for he has Pull'd down his false and lofty Steeple.

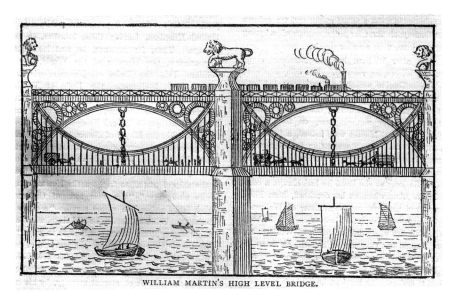

WILLIAM MARTIN'S HIGH LEVEL BRIDGE.

William Martin's idea for a High Level Bridge looks remarkably familiar. Martin claimed Robert Stephenson stole his idea (except for the giant lions).

last ran unaided for more than 20 years). Most importantly, in 1819 he invented a miner's safety lamp which the men of Willington Colliery declared to be better than those of Humphrey Davy and George Stephenson.

Unfortunately, William was no entrepreneur. His inventions were ignored or stolen. His lamp was suppressed. He began to write pamphlets (hundreds of them) denouncing Davy as a murderer or accusing Isaac Newton of being a false prophet, and many others raging against all sorts of 'learned humbugs'. The title alone of his autobiography consists of a 101 words. On his many visits to London he was a great embarrassment to his brother John, who nevertheless 'lent' him money and often drew up designs for his innumerable schemes for salvaging ships, for mine ventilation systems, and for flying machines. He wrote vainly to Prime Ministers and to Queen Victoria for recognition of his genius, and began to describe himself as the 'Philosophical conqueror of all Nations', having discovered that gravity was wrong and that the cause of all things was 'God the first and air the second'. After the death of his long-suffering wife he ended his years in London at his brother's house, to the end versifying, denouncing and inventing. He died in 1851 and epitomises our idea of the grand English eccentric.

❧ *Max Adams*

An anti-hero: Jean Paul Marat – the greatest of all revolutionary journalists

We know that Jean Paul Marat was murdered and died in his bath in his rooms in Paris on 13 July 1793. Whether he ever took a bath during his time in Newcastle we will probably never know. Exactly how he came to be on Tyneside, what he did during two or so years in the North East, where he lived and who he associated with remain to be discovered. There are tantalising fragments and half facts that meld in well with the mystery and myth of his life.

Marat was born in 1743 in the small Swiss town of Boudry, but by the age of 16 he was working in Bordeaux and attending the Faculty of Medicine there. Shortly afterwards he travelled to Paris, but by his own account, wanting to pursue serious study and keep out of trouble (perhaps political trouble), he made his way to Britain in 1765 aged 22.

Marat may have spent time teaching at the Warrington Academy, and he may have moved to Oxford and been responsible for a theft at the Ashmolean Museum in 1768 (but being a highly principled character it is very unlikely that he was the 'Jean Pierre Maitre' who was convicted of the offence). It is reported that, under the name of John White, he taught embroidery in Edinburgh for a time. Debt forced him to flee that city and by 1770 he was in Newcastle where he was arrested but later released. Had he found his way to Hartlepool (where being a Frenchman, or indeed a monkey, could lead to an untimely end) instead, that might have been the end of the story.

The evidence to support any of this is, to say the least, thin, however Jean Paul Marat did arrive in Newcastle and seems to have earned his living working as a vet. He regularly took human patients too and, according to Marat-lore, in recognition of his treatment of the sick of Newcastle, Marat was made an honorary freeman of the town. Any documents that might substantiate this have yet to be uncovered. Certainly Marat wasn't formally qualified or licensed to practise medicine; the degree of Doctor of Medicine later awarded by St Andrews was honorary. However, Marat's brand of quackery must have been relatively successful as in 1777 he was appointed physician to the guard of the Count d'Artois.

Arguably Marat's most famous work was formulated, if

THE

CHAINS OF SLAVERY,

A WORK WHEREIN

THE CLANDESTINE AND VILLAINOUS ATTEMPTS OF

PRINCES TO RUIN LIBERTY

ARE POINTED OUT,

AND THE

DREADFUL SCENES OF DESPOTISM DISCLOSED,

TO WHICH IS PREFIXED,

An ADDRESS to the ELECTORS of GREAT BRITAIN,
in order to draw their TIMELY ATTENTION to the Choice of
proper REPRESENTATIVES in the next PARLIAMENT.

————*Vitam impendere vero.*

LONDON:

Sold by J. ALMON, opposite Burlington House, in Piccadilly; T. PAYNE, at the
Mews Gate; and RICHARDSON & URQUHART, near the Royal Exchange.
MDCCLXXIV,

not written, when he lived in Newcastle. *The Chains of Slavery* was first published – and in English – in 1774. The *Newcastle Public Advertiser* of 3 May published a notice of the work, which went on general sale at ten shillings and sixpence. Later the *Chronicle* announced that the Company of Bricklayers, the Company of Goldsmiths and the Lumber Troop in Newcastle had each been presented with a copy.

During his time in Newcastle, Marat attended a number of the debating clubs and 'Patriotic' societies that met regularly about the town and frequented the premises of the booksellers Charnley, Humble and Slack, as well as Robert Sands' 'circulating library'. Newcastle had established a tradition of radical politics and there were stirrings of unrest among the chattering classes. A great deal of radical, reforming and republican feeling was expressed at many of these gatherings. Marat must have been heartened by this, but ultimately disappointed that it came to very little more than hot air.

Back in Paris in the late 1780s, Marat threw himself totally into the cause of the revolution and was made a Deputy. He tirelessly pursued those he saw as the enemies of the people, almost always calling for their execution. Thousands met their fate at the guillotine as a result. Following his assassination by Charlotte Corday, Marat's body was placed in the Pantheon and a decree was read bestowing 'immortality' on him. In Newcastle it is argued by some that his name passed into the local dialect; Marat became 'marra', the marra (or friend) of the people.

❧ *Douglas Glendinning*

And a thoroughly bad lot – this woman can hardly be described as one of Tyneside's finest, but she was certainly notorious.

Mary Ann Cotton – poisoner

Mary Ann Cotton (born Mary Ann Robson) is probably the region's most notorious serial killer. Any murder is wicked and evil but when we realise she was almost certainly responsible for the deaths by poisoning of at least 17 people, mainly relatives, the horrendous magnitude of her crimes becomes apparent.

Most of the deaths related to her numerous children, who eventually totalled 18 (including six step children). It is thought at least 11 of them died in suspicious circumstances before reaching the age of ten. Mary married on four occasions and three of her husbands also met untimely deaths. Her first marriage took place in 1852 at the Register Office in Castle Garth, Newcastle and the last, bigamously to Frederick Cotton, at St Andrew's Parish Church, Newcastle some 18 years later. Other people who died in questionable circumstances included her mother, a sister-in-law and an 'old flame' who made the fatal mistake of making a will in her favour.

Born in 1832 in a Durham mining village, this ambitious and

charismatic miner's daughter lived at various addresses around in the county as well as in Northumberland and Newcastle. Following a period as a Sunday school teacher she worked mainly as a dressmaker and nurse.

Following many of the deaths suspicion fell on Mary, but there were always other circumstances which stopped action being taken against her. Among these were the huge number of child deaths in the mid-19th century, the ready availability of arsenic for general use and the lack of witnesses due to poisoners' secretive methods. It was never proved Mary dispensed arsenic; she was convicted and hanged in

1873 because abnormally high levels of it found on the body of an exhumed and recent victim gave substance to circumstantial evidence.

The motive for so many unexplained deaths seems to have been Mary's need for money and evidence suggests she usually made sure her intended victims were insured. Though not an apparent alcoholic or gambler, she is known to have had an aversion to housework and may well have been a spendthrift. She probably had delusions of grandeur and repeatedly saw the need to rid herself of dependents whenever they posed a threat to a new and possibly improved lifestyle. Others simply saw her as oversexed; she adored men and they found her attractive with her dark eyes, raven hair and high cheek bones. If, perhaps, she could have avoided pregnancy she may never have considered poisoning as a necessity.

> *Children's rhyme:*
>
> *'Mary Ann Cotton*
> *She's dead and she's rotten*
> *She lies in her bed*
> *With her eyes wide open*
> *Sing, sing, oh what can I sing*
> *Mary Ann Cotton is tied up with string.*
> *Where, where? Up in the air*
> *Sellin' black puddens a penny a pair.'*

Alan Morgan

And the ghost at the Old Assembly Rooms

The Grey Lady of the Old Assembly Rooms, Fenkle Street, is perhaps one of the best known ghost stories associated with Newcastle upon Tyne. The first stone of the Assembly Rooms was laid in 1774 and it was formally opened on 24 June 1776. The money for this prestigious building was donated by 129 prominent North East citizens at £25 a share.

Eighteen months after the opening, on the evening of 31 December 1777, a riotous and drunken party to celebrate the coming New Year was underway in what is now known as the Chandelier Room. One of the more unpleasant guests insisted his wife dance for the assembled crowd – naked! Shamed and stunned by her husband's request, the poor woman was forced to comply, but afterwards, overcome by humiliation, she ran up the spiral staircase to the musicians' balcony and threw herself off, falling to her death in front of the partygoers.

Since that day it has been said that her sad and shamed spectre roams the Assembly Rooms, always accompanied by the scent of lavender and the rustle of silk skirts. The Grey Lady is also sometimes accompanied by the ghost of a dark, heavy-set man who is said to be one of the first owners of the Rooms. In recent years both day and night staff have reported incidents of something unseen brushing past them on the main stairs, of a mischievous presence that blows in the ears of the cleaners, and the odd smell of lavender that appears and disappears. The double doors of the ballroom open and close by themselves. Ghost investigators have much to occupy them.

ੴ *Tony Liddell*

The Assembly Rooms soon after opening in 1776.

Tyneside's finest things

We challenged our contributors to nominate Tyneside's finest things; those items that tell a story about the region's identity. Because of Tyneside's long shipbuilding heritage, ships are close to many people's hearts, and several of the Tyne shipyards' finest products are described here, but this section covers a great diversity of finest things from the drink that is synonymous with Geordie life to a centuries-old loo seat.

Tyneside's finest ships

For many years the shipyards of the Tyne were world famous for producing fine ships using the latest in engineering technology. Many had distinguished careers and some were even household names.

HMS Kelly

There will never be a warship quite like HMS *Kelly*. Her story was one of 20 short glorious months of bravery and personal sacrifice ranking with the greatest in the annals of British naval history. More than anything else the *Kelly* saga exemplified the bond of friendship and mutual respect between the men who built the ships and those who sailed in them.

HMS *Kelly*, named after the Admiral of the Fleet Sir John Kelly, was commissioned just 12 days before the outbreak of World War II. Built at the Hawthorn Leslie Yard at Hebburn, she had many new features: the distribution of her armament, her low sleek line, engine room design, and the novel construction of her strengthened hull.

The battle honours of HMS *Kelly* began with the evacuation of troops from Namsos during which she was divebombed. Her luck held for a few days then, in May 1940, a torpedo crashed into her side, making a hole big enough to drive two double-decker

Hawthorn Leslie workers with officers of HMS Kelly 1940.

HMS Kelly in training.

buses through. Her forward boiler was blown open to the sea and she lay stopped, down by the bows and with a heavy list to starboard. With a caretaker crew of 18, she was towed back to the Tyne by HMS *Bulldog*. The fact that she stayed afloat, though half submerged, during a perilous 90-hour North Sea tow during which she was bombed and attacked, was the greatest possible tribute to the skill of those who built her and those who sailed her. When she limped back to the Hawthorn Leslie yard she was greeted by the cheers of crowds of shipyard workers. 27 of her gallant crew found their last resting place in Hebburn cemetery.

After her long repair the *Kelly* returned to service with a new crew, half of whom had never been to sea before. Her end came during the Crete withdrawal in 1941. Leader of the fifth destroyer flotilla, she was hit by a bomb. Although she started to heel over immediately, her guns kept firing until the encroaching sea washed away first one and then another of the gun crews. Nine officers and 121 men were lost when HMS *Kelly* went down.

Lord Louis Mountbatten was *Kelly*'s only captain; he later described her as 'the happiest ship with the best ship's company I can remember'. He also said: 'Most ships have names that been borne by predecessors over the centuries but the *Kelly* is the only ship to have borne that name and to me she is quite unlike any ship I have served in.'

❧ Ian Wilson

HMS King George V

One of the mightiest warships in the world, the 35,000-ton battleship *King George V* was probably Tyneside's greatest contribution to the strength of the Royal Navy.

Built at Vickers Armstrong's Walker Naval Yard, and launched by King George VI on 21 February 1939, she had a distinguished war career and helped to sink the *Bismarck*, pride of the German navy in 1941.

The keel of *King George V*, the first battleship built on Tyneside since HMS *Nelson* in 1925, was laid down on 1 January 1937, and she was completed in December 1940 at a cost of £8m. Between 2,000 and 3,000 men were engaged on her construction.

There was worldwide interest in the new ship and, after her launch, the Admiralty issued the following statement: 'Her main armament consists of 16 5.5 inch guns in eight turrets. Numerous smaller guns will be mounted ... The machinery will be geared turbines, steam being supplied by oil-fired boilers – the ship will be appreciably faster than the last battleships, *Rodney* and *Nelson* built for the Royal Navy and will carry aircraft accommodated in hangars and flown off by means of a catapult ... Particular attention has been given in the design to protect against gunfire, aerial bombs and mines. The complement of officers and men will be about 1,500 and the amenities of the ship's company will be of the highest standard.'

She left the Tyne in great secrecy in October 1940 at the height of the Blitz, slipping down the mine swept waters of the river in pitch darkness and out to sea. It was so black that the pilot master waiting on the riverside watching for her did not see her pass.

After gallant service, including helping to cover the Allied landings on the mainland of Italy at Salerno, the *King George V* went to the Pacific as part of Task Force 37, helping in the American operations against Okinawa and mainland Japan. She was present at the formal surrender of Japan on 2 September in Tokyo Bay.

After the war she became one of Britain's 'mothball' fleet and was finally broken up at a scrapyard on the Firth of Tay in 1958.

Ian Wilson

Mauretania – The Speaking Ship

The Tyne's largest and most famous passenger liner, *Mauretania*, proved herself many times against the might of the North Atlantic waves. She held the Blue Riband for the fastest Atlantic crossing for an impressive 22 years on the eastward passage and 20 years westward. She regularly notched up averages of around 25 knots.

Mauretania (31,938 gross tons) was built at the Wallsend Shipyard of Swan Hunter & Wigham Richardson. She was launched into the Tyne on September 20 1906 by the Dowager Duchess of Roxburghe. Her huge turbine engines, generating 68,000 horsepower, were built by the Wallsend Slipway & Engineering Company under the direction of its manager, Andrew Laing. These engines were constructed according to principles developed by Tyne-based steam turbine inventor Sir Charles Parsons.

The 790ft-long ship was completed in the autumn of 1907, leaving the Tyne for delivery to the Cunard Line in Liverpool on October 22 1907. She was cheered all the way to the sea by thousands of onlookers.

Mauretania shown in her completed colours, based on a photograph taken as she left the Tyne on her preliminary trials in September 1907.

Mauretania left Liverpool on her maiden voyage to New York on November 16 1907 and immediately captured the Blue Riband for the eastward crossing with a speed of 23.69 knots. In September 1909 *Mauretania* won the westward honour with a speed of 26.06 knots and then held on to the Blue Riband for both directions until 1929.

During the First World War *Mauretania* put in sterling service both as a troop ship and hospital ship. In her last years, from around 1930 onwards, she was increasingly used as a cruise liner.

On her final voyage – to the breaker's yard on the shores of the Firth of Forth in 1935 – *Mauretania* halted off the mouth of the Tyne to say farewell to the hard-working people who had built her. Thousands of people turned out to wave her goodbye.

A wireless telegraph message was sent from the ship to the Lord Mayor of Newcastle. For the first time in her life *Mauretania* actually spoke. The message from the Tyne's best-loved liner read: 'Thank you for your greeting. For 28 years I have striven to be a credit to you, and now my day is done. Though I pass on, may Tyneside ever reach out to further and greater triumphs. With pride and affection I greet you. Farewell – *Mauretania*.' It was an extraordinary ending to an extraordinary career.

✤ Ken Smith

The Original

Today, the lifeboat and the RNLI (Royal National Lifeboat Institution) epitomise selfless, voluntary service in the face of maritime danger. It is quite surprising to discover that this humanitarian lifesaving service is a relatively recent innovation. The word 'lifeboat', or 'life-boat', seems to date from first appearance of such boats on Tyneside around the year 1789.

The story of the origins of these first lifeboats, or more accurately Shields lifeboats, has been told and re-told with varying degrees of partisanship for around 200 years. At its simplest it is a tale of a lowly-born Shields eccentric, Willie Wouldhave, who invents a life-saving boat but gains nothing from his brainchild other than the accolades of the ordinary folk of Shields. In reality, the South Shields dignitaries who organised and judged the well-advertised competition that Wouldhave entered: '[to produce] a boat calculated to 'preserve lives',

The Original, first purpose-built lifeboat in the world.

were plainly, and justifiably unhappy with his proposal, although they offered him one guinea – half of the prize. Rubbing (sea) salt into Wouldhave's wounds, in 1789 they commissioned a self-publicising but experienced local boatbuilder, Henry Greathead (whose own design had also been rejected by the competition's judges), to build a dedicated lifesaving boat for them. Although the boat he produced seems to have featured elements from other designs, including Wouldhave's, Greathead quickly claimed the invention of this 'Life-boat' for himself, thereby gaining national celebrity and – even more contentiously – reaping a sizeable cash award from parliament.

The *Original*, the 30-foot, oar-powered boat which Greathead built did great things in the hands of local pilots and fishermen. It saved hundreds of lives, especially around the mouth of the Tyne and along the North East coast. But a sense of injustice remained, causing controversy even when, in 1889, South Shields Borough Council built a fine new monument to celebrate the lifeboat's centenary. Indeed, there are those who continue this Wouldhave v. Greathead argument even today.

Why then should this controversial Greathead-built 'Life-Boat' be considered as Tyneside's finest maritime invention? The answer is simple. It was conceived through humanitarian rather than purely selfish motives and sought to improve the seafarer's lot in an era in which – through warfare and avarice – his life was cheap. It also left a lasting legacy to ships in distress.

❧ *Adrian Osler*

The SS QED – the finest early iron ship

Although the *John Bowes* is usually recognised as the first steam collier, I contend that the SS *QED*, built by John Coutts of Low Walker eight years earlier in 1844, showed the way in terms of innovative ideas. One of Coutts' innovations was the use of sealed tanks to contain water as ballast, which was essential to colliers (steam or sail powered) as they returned, usually empty, to their coal loading port.

The *QED* was iron-hulled and barque-rigged, with an auxiliary steam engine to assist passages up the Seine estuary on coal voyages. She had a useful working life of 11 years, even going transatlantic on occasion.

Coutts was an Aberdonian entrepreneur who flashed across the Tyne shipbuilding scene between 1840 and 1855 before failing and dying into obscurity in North Shields in 1862. His vessels included some of the largest iron sailing ships of the day – only in recent years has his contribution to shipbuilding been analysed and appreciated.

Ron French

Turbinia

Turbinia, Charles Parsons' revolutionary 'ocean greyhound', is my favourite ship and has been since I was a child. I see her regularly in her splendid location at Newcastle's Discovery Museum. However, I remember when just a short length of her bow was on display in the

Turbinia shows off her speed on the Tyne in the 1890s.

Science and Engineering Museum in Exhibition Park, and the rest of the ship was part of the collection of the Science Museum in London.

In 1959 the powers that be at the Science Museum decided that they needed the space occupied by their portion of *Turbinia*, so we could have it back. The Wallsend Slipway made a new piece of hull to join the two sections together and the complete vessel was housed in an annexe to the Exhibition Park museum which opened to the public in 1961. By this time I was a sea-going engineer and had more than a passing interest in this historic exhibit. Although I admire immensely the engineering achievement embodied in *Turbinia*, I would not have liked to sail in her. The engine room is rather cramped and her behaviour in a seaway would not have agreed with my stomach.

In 1995 she was moved by road (an interesting spectacle) to the Discovery Museum.

John Dobson

Turbinia's stern section crosses the Tyne Bridge in 1960 on her way to the Museum of Science and Engineering in Exhibition Park, where she would be soon be a source of fascination for many children.

Monuments and memorials

Tyneside has many monuments commemorating the people who lived and worked here. While some of these people are nationally (and even internationally) known, others enjoyed only short-lived fame and, without their monuments, might already have been forgotten.

Newcastle's blue plaques

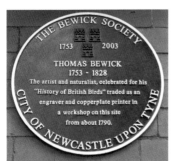

There are about a hundred blue plaques in and around Newcastle and they mark everything from medieval monuments to the home of a Portuguese author. The list includes the Castle Keep; the substantial remains of the town's historic walls; several bridges; the finest works of Tyneside's most famous architect, John Dobson; the achievements of George and Robert Stephenson; the home and office of Richard Grainger; the site of Thomas Bewick's house and studio; the birthplace of Lord Collingwood, the victor of Trafalgar and Nelson's friend and comrade; the home of the renowned naturalists John and Albany Hancock; the house in which Ludwig Wittgenstein, one of the world's leading 20th century thinkers, lived; and the music hall where Charles Dickens gave his many performances in Newcastle.

They celebrate some of the city's most famous; Lord Taylor of Gosforth, former Lord Chief Justice of England and Wales; Dr Gibb, the physician immortalised in the song *The Blaydon Races*; the painters Ralph Hedley and William Bell Scott; miners' leader and first working-class MP, Thomas Burt; authors Sid Chaplin and Jack Common; musicians Charles Avison and William Rea; engineer Ove Arup; Cardinal Basil Hume; Gladstone Adams, inventor of the windscreen wiper; and Tyneside's first Olympian, Alec Burns.

Begun by Tyne and Wear County Council in the late 1970s and continued by Newcastle City Council, the city's commemorative plaque scheme celebrates the amazing historic, architectural and cultural diversity of the city. How can this impressive but disparate collection of Newcastle's great historic buildings, heritage sites and famous sons (no daughters as yet) be compared to each other to arrive at the city's

finest? They obviously cannot and so instead I offer my completely arbitrary awards for the city's finest plaques.

In third place, the Most Exotic Plaque award goes to 53 Grey Street – 'Jose Maria de Eca de Queiros 1845-1900 Portuguese diplomat and novelist of European stature lived in this building 1874-1879, among the most productive years of his writing career.' Eca is renowned throughout Europe, particularly in Portugal where he is regarded as the country's Dickens. Jose Maria de Eca de Queiros is certainly the most exotic name to grace any of the City's plaques and his presence testifies to the little known cosmopolitan nature of 19th century Newcastle.

In second place, the award for the Plaque with the Most Global Significance goes to the Stephenson Works at 20 South Street, behind Central Station which marks the site at which *Rocket*, *Locomotion* and a host of other early pioneering locomotives were born and given to the world. The development of the locomotive and, with it, the modern railway was of undoubted global significance. Robert Stephenson & Sons deserves its place in history.

20 South Street, the Stephenson Works.

In first place, the Award for the Plaque with Sheer Class goes to that to Yevgeny Zamyatin (1884-1937) on Sanderson Road in Jesmond. Zamyatin came to Newcastle from Russia in 1916, worked in the Tyne shipyards as a naval architect, designed ice-breakers, wrote two satirical novellas, one of which, *Islanders*, lampooned Jesmond society, returned to Russia and wrote the book, *We*, which inspired one of the seminal works of 20th century fiction, Orwell's *1984* – fantastic!

Martin Seymour-Smith in *Who's Who in Twentieth century Literature*, describes *We* as 'one of the truly great novels of the 20th century. *We* burns the mind like dry ice. As a dystopian nightmare it remains unequalled.'

Yevgeny Zamyatin – What a man ! What a Plaque! What a Scrabble score!

❦ Ian Ayris

Grey's Monument

Few men have had a monument as magnificent as Grey's monument erected in their lifetime. Charles, Earl Grey of Howick was the initiator of the 1832 Reform Bill and Prime Minister from 1830 to 1834.

In 1836 a group of the Earl's friends and admirers suggested a public subscription to pay for a memorial to him in Newcastle. A committee invited proposals for the design of the monument. Twelve schemes were submitted, among them designs from the architect, John Green, and from his nephew, also John. Although there were many objections over the need for a monument, its form and its location, John Green senior was eventually chosen as architect. His son Benjamin worked with him. In September 1836 Green invited tenders for 'the Building of a COLUMN in Newcastle upon Tyne as a Memorial to EARL GREY' to specifications available at his office in the Royal Arcade. The successful contractors were John and Joseph Welch, who had also built Bellingham Bridge. One year later work began.

Originally intended to have been higher, the fluted Roman Doric column was built to a height of 133 feet and a twice-life-size statue of Grey was commissioned from Edward Hodges Baily, of London. Work

A photograph from the 1860s shows off the relatively new monument to Earl Grey on a muddy Grey Street.

on the shaft began in March 1838, and by August of the same year the 1,350 ton masonry column had been completed and the statue placed in position. At the same time Upper Dean Street was renamed Grey Street.

The 'Grey Column' was not received by Newcastle's inhabitants with great enthusiasm. Even during building the critics raised objections; it should have been sited on the Town Moor; a triumphal arch would have been better; an educational establishment would have been more useful; would the chimneys of the region's alkali works compete with the column? It was also difficult to raise funds for construction. Perhaps the ultimate insult was that Grey himself, although still alive but said not to be popular, did not attend either the stone-laying or the completion ceremonies.

Despite these early setbacks, over the years the monument has endeared itself to Geordies and has become an icon for the city.

Robert W. Rennison

The Stephenson Monument

When J.G. Lough's statue to George Stephenson near the Central Station was officially unveiled in 1862 more than 100,000 people were present. They were there to venerate the memory of one of the greatest of all North Easterners – a man whose engineering genius transformed the world and yet who needed a translator to help members of parliament penetrate his Geordie accent when he went to London to report to a parliamentary committee.

Crowds surround the Stephenson Monument at its unveiling, 2 October, 1862.

His genius is thoroughly represented on his statue. Seated around the plinth on which he stands are four figures representing the various fields of skill in which he excelled. There's a miner, a locomotive engineer, a blacksmith and a plate layer, though, to be honest I'm not sure the characterisation would reveal what they were if the figures weren't holding the tools of their trade on their laps. Often, of course, they also hold other things to show their regional identity – bottles of Brown Ale, for example, and in this globalised age, cans of Australian lager.

Round about this statue are some of the greatest buildings in Newcastle.

There's the Central Station, John Dobson's masterwork and a suitable reminder of Newcastle's pre-eminent role in the industrial revolution. There's the Lit and Phil (the first art gallery in the world to be lit by gas and to stay open in the evening) with the lecture room where Sir Joseph Swan first demonstrated the possibilities of the incandescent electric light bulb.

There's the beautiful medieval St John's Church, a glorious haven of peace from the city's noise and all around there are buildings which perfectly illustrate the shift and flow of architectural style and the wealth of the Victorian City. It's a wonderful place – and yet …

If that crowd of 100,000 people were to try and look at the statue nowadays vast numbers of them would be knocked down by taxis swooping round it on their way to the station or rushing past to deliver drunks to the Quayside. Road markings and traffic lights, pedestrian crossings and road signs complete the picture. Twentieth century buildings of mind-numbing ordinariness overpower the great monuments of the past. It is a sad state of affairs that such a wonderful and iconic object should have become a thing, a lost thing on a traffic island. It's time, I think, to recognise its beauty and the huge significance of its surroundings and restore the whole space to something like its former glory.

❧ *John Grundy*

Jesmond Old Cemetery

An air of mystery seems to be what most visitors experience as they approach the impressive but solemn main entrance of the cemetery. Perhaps they wonder what lies within the high stone wall that surrounds it. Once inside, its appeal is heightened by an apparently haphazard layout, with interesting mounds here and there, mixed trees and shrubs and a lack of formal paths.

Its many memorials range from the rather modest original headstone for John Dobson, the renowned local architect, simply inscribed 'JD', to the huge and elaborate gothic monument to Archibald Reed. They often give the occupations of the grave's inhabitants together with other snippets of social history. The cemetery is the last resting place for many of Newcastle's famous residents.

Dobson's massive gates to Jesmond Old Cemetery.

Opened in 1836 as a private cemetery, it offered a dignified alternative to Newcastle's parish churchyards which were grossly overcrowded, unhealthy and largely restricted to members of the Church of England. Though more expensive than the parish churchyard it did offer advantages including provision for most religious groups, a more dignified burial service, adequate security (with a high wall to deter grave robbers), a choice of plot and perhaps most importantly a permanent resting place. It also had catacombs under the chapels where bereaved families could rent a secure stone shelf as a temporary resting place before the funeral as an as an alternative to keeping the coffin and its inhabitant in the family home. The chapels and catacombs are no longer used for their original purpose and are closed to the public.

John Dobson designed the buildings in the fashionable Classical style and landscaped the cemetery.

❧ *Alan Morgan*

Tyneside's finest tombstone – the Regina tombstone

Romans wanted to be remembered after they were dead, and so those who could afford it had a tombstone set up over their grave. Some of the stones simply contained inscriptions, giving name and family, sometimes age at death and the name of the person who set up the tombstone for them. Others had an image of the deceased carved in the stone, often shown in everyday scenes such as being served a drink by a slave, or eating a meal with their family. The Regina tombstone from Arbeia, South Shields Roman Fort, has both inscription and image, and it is a delight because of the amount of information that it

contains.

The inscription records a tale of love, travel and tragedy, raising many questions which can never now be answered. A man called Barates came to Britain from a city called Palmyra in Syria, bringing a female slave called Regina from a British tribe in the south. At some point Barates freed Regina and married her, and they travelled to one of the most distant parts of the Empire, near Hadrian's Wall, to work. And here, aged only 30, Regina died.

Barates commissioned the magnificent tombstone from a fellow Syrian living nearby, and under the Latin inscription asked for a line in his own language, Aramaic, to be added: 'Regina, freedwoman of Barates, alas'. This is the typical form of Syrian tombstone inscription, and this bi-lingual tombstone, the only one from Roman Britain, reflects a fusing of different traditions in the cosmopolitan mix of the area 1,800 years ago.

The detailed relief shows Regina sitting in a comfortable wicker chair, holding a distaff and spindle for spinning thread in one hand. A basket full of balls of spun wool to one side of the chair is a symbol of her industry. On the other side of the chair is a box with metal fittings and a lock; Regina is lifting the lid to show to the viewer the treasures within. Her wealth is also reflected in the gown she is wearing (a fashion only very recently introduced from the Continent) as well as in her hairstyle set in waves like a 1920s perm, and in the jewellery at her neck and wrists. Regina, the slave called 'Queen', had come a long way in her short life.

Alex Croom

Mark Armstrong's gravestone, Christ Church, North Shields

The lines on Mark Armstrong's gravestone (see over the page) refer to the story of the seamen's strike of January 1851. It arose from the Mercantile Marine Act which sought to regulate wages and shipping offices. Seamen on the Tyne attempted to prevent ships crewed by men willing to accept lower wages from leaving the river. On 11th February ten men, including Mark Armstrong, were taken into custody for attempting to persuade the crew of the *Huntcliff* to abandon ship but were discharged in the absence of the chief witness for the prosecution. On 16th February five watchers in a boat trying to stop ships

going to sea collided with the ship's boat while going alongside. Their boat capsized and Mark Armstrong was drowned. At the coroner's inquest the verdict was 'accidental death'. Armstrong was buried at Christ Church graveyard on 19th February, with 1,000 seamen accompanying the cortege. The strike was settled two days later.

Erected to the memory of Mark Armstrong of North Shields, Mariner aged 25
Who was drowned in the river Tyne 16th Feb 1851,
while exerting himself with his Brother SEAMEN
during the Great Struggle for the Rights and Freedom
of British SEAMEN.
This memorial is placed here by his Brother SEAMEN
and a few friends in North and South Shields,
Tynemouth & their [sic] Vicinities as a mark of
Respect.
I am anchored here below with many of our fleet,
But once again we must set sail our Admiral Christ to
meet.

At the foot of the stone is carved an upturned boat.

Constance Fraser

South African War Memorial, Haymarket – dulce et decorum est

Born in Ashington in the days when we had an Empire, and having served in the former Royal Northumberland Fusiliers as a National Serviceman in the regular battalion, and later in a territorial battalion, I have always been fascinated by things military. Even now, in the twilight of my life, I am still, as my dear wife says, army barmy! Living as I do, north of Newcastle upon Tyne, I am always impressed, as I enter the city, by the magnificent, towering South African War Memorial standing on Barras Bridge. To me it epitomises the graceful artistry of the Edwardian period. It is a smack in the eye to those who vandalised Newcastle in the 1960s with their concrete boxes. A beautiful tribute to those men of Newcastle and the County of Northumberland who lost their lives in that far land over 100 years ago.

It was financed by money from the Northumberland War Fund which had been raised at the start of the war (1899 to 1902). A competition was set up and 41 models were submitted. The winner was T. Eyre Macklin, RBA, of Newcastle. His design features a 68 feet high six-sided obelisk on a base. On the summit of this tapering column stands an imposing figure of winged Victory, ten feet tall; her left hand rests on her sword, while in her right hand she holds a the victor's wreath. In touching contrast to her dignity and impassiveness is the tenderness expressed is the beautifully modelled figure at the base, which represents a draped female form holding a palm branch. She is Northumbria, paying her tribute to her fallen sons, although she is sometimes said to portray 'Sorrow mourning her loss'. On bronze

The Haymarket and the War Memorial around 1910, no traffic, no Metro station.

shields at the base of the monolith, joined together by garlands of oak leaves, are inscribed the names of the officers, non-commissioned officers, and soldiers who laid down their lives for the honour of their county. Underneath the figures are the words: *Dulce et decorum est pro patria mori.*

The obelisk and base were constructed of stone provided by Lord Armstrong from his quarries at Cragside, near Rothbury, in Northumberland. They were constructed by J.C. Ferguson, of Newcastle. The bronze castings were by Messieurs Montaculltelli Frères, of Gentiley sur Seine, France.

The memorial cost around £2,000. It was officially unveiled on 22 June 1908, by Lieutenant-General Sir Laurence Oliphant KCVO, CB, Commander-in-Chief of Northern Command.

There are 110 names of men from the volunteer units of Newcastle and Northumberland, and 241 officers and soldiers of the two regular battalions of The Northumberland Fusiliers. The volunteer units shown on the shields are the Northumberland and Durham Yeomanry (Northumberland Hussars); 5th (Militia) Battalion, Northumberland Fusiliers; Elswick Battery, 1st Newcastle Royal Garrison (Volunteers); Newcastle Royal Engineers, (1st Volunteers); 1st, 2nd, & 3rd (Volunteer) Battalions, the Northumberland Fusiliers.

Thomas Hewitson

The Response – pro patria mori

There are many war memorials across Tyneside. Several commemorate the men who served in the Boer War, such as the towering figure of Winged Victory in the Haymarket in Newcastle and the winged figure of Peace in Saltwell Park in Gateshead.

One of the most evocative Second Word War memorials is in Mill Dam, South Shields. It represents a sailor at a ship's wheel on a tilting deck in remembrance of the merchant navy men who lost their lives.

The need to make some kind of sense of, and express a profound grief over the unprecedented mass slaughter of the First World War,

NON SIBI SED PATRIAE
THE RESPONSE 1914

resulted in memorials in virtually every community. Newcastle's Old Eldon Square has the imposing memorial featuring St George and the Dragon, unveiled by Earl Haigh, but fronting Newcastle Civic Centre is the most eloquent of them all. The Response, by sculptor William Goscombe John, depicts a column of soldiers answering the call to arms. Made in black bronze, it illustrates the fervour and patriotism which marked the start of what would become a war of unspeakable horror.

The procession is headed by drummer boys. Some of the men turn to say their farewells to wives and children. Soaring above their heads is the figure of Renown, blowing a raised trumpet. It is based on the march to war of the 5th Northumberland Fusiliers from their camp in Gosforth Park, Newcastle, through the Haymarket and on to the Central Station, with the streets lined with people.

The memorial was commissioned by Tyneside shipowner Sir George Renwick and his wife, partly in thanks for the safe return of their five sons from the battlefields.

It was unveiled by the Prince of Wales in July, 1923. On the same day he visited St James's Park to watch 42,000 children stage a display of red, white and blue flags in a variety of combinations.

Tony Henderson

The necessities of life

A pudding, a pint ... and another thing

Newcastle Pudding

Broth, pease pudding (originally pea pudding but someone thought it ought to have an 's') stotty cake, leek pudding and Singing Hinnies are traditional North East delicacies, but I can find no evidence that any of them originated on Tyneside.

In the course of researching and writing a book of Northumbrian recipes I could find only one that possibly related solely to Tyneside. In every book I consulted there were references to Newcastle Pudding. This appeared to be a simple bread and butter pudding varied by the addition of lemon or lemon juice in some form or another in the pudding itself or in the sauce. I could find no reason why it was called Newcastle Pudding or why, in an area where cooking was based firstly on the availability of ingredients and secondly on bulking food to be as filling as possible without sacrificing the flavour, there should be a recipe using such an unusual ingredient as lemons. We take lemons (and all exotic fruit) for granted nowadays but, until comparatively recently, lemons were usually available only during the winter months and had to be preserved in some form for the remainder of the year (a problem with all citrus fruits – woe betide the cook who did not make sufficient marmalade during the brief season of the Seville orange).

I was unable to find any explanation of this but decided Newcastle Pudding was too good a recipe to omit, especially when we had a delightful and witty illustration produced by Anne Curtis to accompany it.

Several slices of stale bread
butter
the rind of one lemon
3 tbsps sugar
2 eggs
1 pint of milk

Butter a 1 pint basin and half fill it with the slices of buttered bread. Sprinkle sugar and peel between each layer (you could also add some dried fruit if you wished or a pinch of mixed spice). Beat the eggs lightly and mix carefully with the warmed (not too hot) milk. If you like a stronger lemon flavour you can add more peel to the milk as you warm it and then let it stand a while before mixing it with the eggs and pouring it over the bread. Cover with two layers of greaseproof paper or foil and steam for one hour. Serve with cream, lemon sauce, or custard. This may also be made in a pie dish and cooked in a moderate to hot oven.

Over the years I have given various talks on Northumbrian recipes which led to me discovering one further snippet about Newcastle Pudding. At the end of a talk a lady came up to me and said that she never under any circumstances made her bread and butter pudding with lemons. The starting point for her mother's bread and butter pudding had been to soak the bread in lemon juice. She herself hated this and had never used the recipe once she had her own kitchen. Her mother came from Middlesbrough!!

Barbara Stephenson

Newcastle Brown Ale

A bottled beer once regarded, albeit unfairly, as the preserve of those of pensionable age now sells nearly 100 million litres worldwide. This remarkable success story is even more impressive when we consider that Tyneside was never a leading brewing centre: Newcastle's national reputation in drinking circles rested on its high position in the drunkenness leagues and alcohol consumption tables.

Newcastle Brown Ale was first put before the public in 1927, after three years' development by Newcastle Breweries' head brewer Colonel James Porter and chief chemist Arthur Jones. It went on sale at ninepence a pint and, one year later, collected the Brewers' Exhibition Challenge Cup for the best bottled beer at the International Brewers' Exhibition. In those days Newcastle Brown Ale was a peculiarly northern delicacy, said to have been created to match the palates of those in heavy industry, with a higher than normal salt content. Today's product differs little from Colonel Porter's creation: a reddish brown beer with more caramel than hop flavour and a nutty aftertaste, delivered in a clear flint glass bottle.

Long-standing aficionados of Newcastle Brown Ale thought it best drunk by decanting it at regular intervals into a Wellington (a particular shape and size of glass, not a gumboot) but by 1962 it had made its debut in cans, allowing small consignments to find their way to exiles abroad. The beer often turned up in charity auctions where sentimental Tynesiders lost some sense of proportion: in the 1970s, for example, a lecturer at Kadunh Polytechnic sold a single can for 116 Nigerian niara, the equivalent of £70.

Newcastle Brown Ale's growing popularity took off in the 1980s as a younger generation discovered the uniqueness of its taste and appearance, aided perhaps by the fact that the beer has always been served colder than other traditional ales. By the middle of the decade, inroads were also being made into export markets. With the arrival of the new millennium, a loss of marketing nerve saw the word ale – thought to be dangerously old-fashioned – removed from promotional material, but it was eventually restored. The global impact of Newcastle Brown Ale is such that it is now available in 40 countries and has been granted the European Union's Protection of Geographical Indications status, joining the ranks of Jersey Royal potatoes and Parma Ham in earning protection from imitations. But these days Newcastle Brown Ale, as with much of Tyneside's iconic cultural output, is produced in the Borough of Gateshead.

✤ Brian Bennison

A Roman latrine seat – possibly Tyneside's chilliest loo

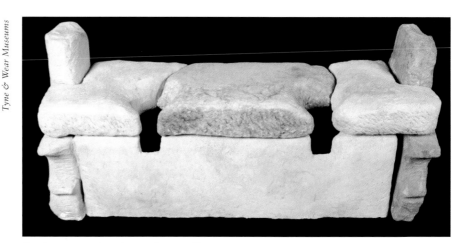

Latrine seat at Segedunum Roman Fort.

Imagine the scene: it's mid-afternoon on a winter's day and it's already grown dark outside. You can hear the wind whistling round the building, and the sound of the rain dripping off the eaves. You are a soldier, safe and sound in a warm hospital, recovering from some winter sickness that has left you drained and without any reserves of strength. You need to go to the toilet, but thankfully, because this is a hospital, there is a latrine built into a corner room and there is no need to use a chamber-pot in your room or venture out through the icy drizzle to a building built against the fort wall. Candle in hand, you shuffle into the multi-seater latrine that can hold eight patients if need be. You sit down, and promptly discover the seat is stone. Freezing cold stone against your bare skin.

Part of one such stone latrine seat has been found at Segedunum Roman Fort. Multi-seater latrines are well known from Roman sites such as Housesteads and Arbeia, and reconstructions have appeared on thousands of postcards and posters, but while the drains and sometimes the seat supports survive, the seating rarely does as it was made of wood. Stone seating, often of marble, is known from elsewhere in the Empire, but very few examples are known from this country, and this is the best example of them all. It is not treasure and it is not beautiful, no-one famous used it or made it, but archaeology is all about learning the details of people's lives in the past, and you cannot get more every-day than a toilet seat.

❧ Alex Croom

Tyneside's finest secrets

Tyneside is full of secrets; some buried deep underground and others that you might pass every day without noticing.

The mysterious cross in the pavement

One of the best things about our towns is that you are always discovering something you hadn't noticed before.

Take, for example, the little cross carved into the paving of the mini-piazza in front of the Theatre Royal in Grey Street. Have you noticed it? Why not? It's been quietly lying there minding its own business since the 12th April 2000, the day it was unveiled by a horde of enthusiastic school children, aided and abetted by the Lord Mayor of Newcastle, the Chair of the Grainger Town Partnership and the Project Officer of the North East Environmental Education Forum, the educational organisation that organised the event as well as the carving of the cross.

So what is this all about? What is the pavement cross for? Why is it important for Tyneside?

Well, quite simply, the cross is the permanent marker of the burial place of the Grainger Town Children's Millennium Capsule under Grey Street, appropriately in the heart of our great Northern city. For weeks and weeks, children and staff from Walbottle First School, Canning Street Primary School and Trinity School – Oakfield Collage, laboured to produce wonderful Grainger Town poems, tapes, drawings, stories and pictures to go into the capsule. The pile of material grew day by day, well beyond the physical capacity of the modest burial container. Hard choices had to be made but, finally, the material that did not go into the capsule was displayed in the Central Library and in Waterstone's shop window for everyone to enjoy.

I had suggested, on the old principle that 'X always marks the spot', that the cross carved into the pavement should take the form of a cartoon pirate cross, like the ones you find on the average treasure map. Artist Simon Watkinson, who was advising on the Theatre Royal lighting at the time, had a better idea: a carving in the form of the cheap sticky plastic crosses traditionally applied to the stage to show the principle actors where to stand, surrounded by an ellipse which represents the spotlight falling onto the stage.

So Tyneside has the only floodlit sticky-back-plastic stone cross in the World!

It gets better; the official scroll, recording the unveiling event, explains:

'It is expected that in 25 years time on 12th April 2025, the capsule will be exhumed in the presence of the same children who witnessed its burial and its contents then displayed for the enjoyment and enlightenment of school children of that time.'

You are all invited to join me at this event. See you in 2025!

David Lovie

Stone, terracotta and marble – the devil is in the detail

St Nicholas' Cathedral.

Across the city are many fine examples of architectural enrichment of buildings, churches and townscape. Many of these sculptures, plaques and statues are made of various kinds of stone, and occasionally terracotta. They are often finely detailed, such as the carving of the spire of St Nicholas' Cathedral which is found on a plaque in St Nicholas' cemetery. Nearby are roughly carved empty stone coffins. Another coffin, this time an early representation, carved in stone, with a skeleton peeping out of it can be seen in St Andrew's churchyard.

Inside St Nicholas' Cathedral you will find the Lloyd Memorial, designed by local architects Oliver and Leeson and carved by F. W. Pomeroy. The modern

The memorial to John Collingwood Bruce.

Atlantes support the 29 Collingwood Street balcony.

Terracotta infants on Grey Street.

Communion Sculpture by Stephen Cox representing the Communion wafer and wine is made of Roman Imperial Porphyry and Egyptian alabaster. There is a monument of painted marble erected in memory of Henry Maddison who died in 1634. Also in the cathedral look out for the marble effigy of John Collingwood Bruce whose feet rest on an open book: his own work on the Roman Wall.

There are fascinating details wherever you look. Over the door at 23-29 Collingwood Street carved Atlantes (more than one Atlas) support a balcony. Down on the Quayside, Neptune and Fishwives (by the sculptor George Burns) grace the old Fishmarket. On Wallknoll or Sallyport Tower, which was the meeting hall of the Guild of Ships' Carpenters, is a carved relief of a ship's hull. Can you spot the terracotta figures of infants in Grey Street and Mosley Street?

❧ *Thomas Yellowley*

Stone coffins at St Nicholas' Cathedral.

A goat leers down from the old medical school, College Street.

A ship on Sallyport Tower, City Road.

Gravestone at St Andrew's Churchyard.

'Labor and wait': a fine North East tradition

In Chinatown's Stowell Street, a brick building next to the corner pub has in its gable a beautifully-carved wheatsheaf over the motto 'Labor and wait'. Below, helpfully, is '1908'. What was this all about?

The situation gives the first clue, the motto the second, and the date the third. First, it is just round the corner from the Co-op's shop in Newgate Street. Second, the wheatsheaf was the emblem and the words were the motto of the Co-operative Wholesale Society, which revolutionised shopping for the working classes. (I have found no explanation for the use of the American spelling, 'Labor'.) And third, knowing the date of a building makes it much easier to learn more about it.

Anna Flowers

There was a CWS shop in Newgate Street by 1870; it extended into Darn Crook in the following decades. In the 1930s the entire front range was replaced (in two phases so that the shop never closed) with a fine art déco building – look at those staircase windows and handrails! The new work had not extended around the corner into Darn Crook, but one of those older shops still has a scrap of 1930s frieze with waves of blue glass.

The more humble building in Stowell Street was a warehouse for 'green fruit' (according to the application made to the City Council in 1907 by L.G. Ekins, the CWS architect, which is still in Tyne and Wear Archives). Mr Jim Lamb has kindly told me that it was a greengrocery warehouse. It was enlarged in 1927, to make room for a 'banana ripening warehouse'. According to the plans all the masonry had to be an exact copy of the earlier building. Ventilation was through a louvred turret in the roof. What happened when wartime restrictions did not allow the import of bananas? People just laboured, and waited.

Grace McCombie

Hidden treasures on the streets

Photos TY

A horse on a Dean Street grating.

Hidden away in the streets of Newcastle there are some fine examples of street furniture from a bygone age. Outside the castle keep is a horse-mounting block for those not agile enough to mount a horse unaided, or women with long skirts. It was also helpful for loading carts. Across the road in Castle Garth you will find a few old wooden cobbles, useful for sound reduction in the days of metal cartwheels. Similar wooden cobbles can be seen outside the Station Hotel in Neville Street.

Another type of street furniture was the marker. In City Road there is an unusual cast iron ordnance survey marker while in Forth Lane there is a plaque boundary marker with three castles. Occasionally we find engraved marks in the granite kerbstones indicating where electricity cables entered a property; some of these can be seen in Northumberland Road.

Boundary marker, City Road.

Bollards (also called stumps or carriage posts) are another common type of street furniture designed to protect buildings or statues, or to bar traffic from lanes and cul de sacs. They are still popular with traffic engineers today. Several early examples can be found around the city and they come in various shapes, sizes and designs. The example shown is in the Central Station entrance.

The Penfold letter box was designed by J.W. Penfold. Known as Hexagonal Penfolds, they were put up between 1866 and 1879 and had a sort of acanthus leaf on the dome, with or without a finial. The first one cost £7.18s.3d. The only example in Newcastle is in Osborne Avenue, Jesmond.

Another reminder of the past is the cast iron cover manufactured by Smith Patterson's of Blaydon for the Corporation Tramway, which can be seen in an alley on the quayside. While on the quayside look out for bollards and rings for the tethering of ships.

✤ Thomas Yellowley

Shell-shaped bollards at the Central Station.

Keep your eyes open for hidden history in Newcastle's street furniture.

Wooden cobbles, Castle Garth.

Penfold letter box, Osborne Avenue, Jesmond.

Newcastle's three castles, Forth Lane.

Even after we discount the numerous mine works which perforate subterranean Tyneside, there are still more tunnels than many people realise, and perhaps some that we remain unaware of; a 'new' old tunnel was exposed about a dozen years ago which seemed to lead down to the Tyne from just behind the cemetery at the top of Westgate Hill in Newcastle.

The modern Metro tunnels and the Tyne road tunnel are of course well known, the 1842 Victoria Tunnel is now more widely appreciated, and many will recall the Quayside Branch railway tunnel of 1870 which closed in 1969. Fewer people will be familiar with Kitty's Drift, a three-mile-long horse-drawn waggonway tunnel of 1796 from Kenton colliery to Bells Close on the Tyne, which became quite a tourist feature in the early 19th century. Fewer still realise that a Tyne Tunnel was built between Carville and Hebburn in around 1904-7, a mere six feet in diameter and designed to carry electricity cables. And perhaps only a handful of people are aware that a tunnel ran, and presumably still runs, from the long-gone North Elswick Pit in Pitt Street just to the

The escalators to the Tyne cycle and pedestrian tunnels were the longest in the world at the time of opening in 1951.

west of St James' Park, down to coal staiths at South Elswick.

But none of these tunnels, all special in their own way, deserves the accolade of Tyneside's finest. That compliment must go to the twin cycle and pedestrian tunnels under the Tyne between Jarrow and Howden. Designed by Mott, Hay & Anderson, with Charles Brand & Son as contractors, the two 900 feet-long tunnels were constructed at 40 feet below the river bed, one of 10 feet diameter for pedestrians, the other of 12 feet diameter for cyclists. Construction began in June 1947 and the tunnels were formally opened on 24 July 1951. The approach escalators, with 85 feet vertical descent, were the longest continuous escalators in the world at the time, and the first anywhere to permit use by people accompanied by bicycles. There are also vertical lifts for prams and services. The tile-lined tunnel interiors were described by *Newcastle Journal*, at the time of their opening, as a 'cream and green highway'.

What makes these tunnels 'Tyneside's finest' is not just the engineering involved, nor the clean lines and functionality of the domed terminal buildings, nor even the splendid wooden escalators, but the sheer enjoyment which they afford when travelling through them, preferably by bicycle. Freewheel where you can, and listen to the hum of your tyres; experience your movement through cool still air; and don't feel reluctant to shout out with joy at midpoint and hear your voice reverberate and echo through 900 feet of tunnel some 40 feet below the bed of the river.

Stafford M. Linsley

Newcastle timepieces

Not strictly a clock but the Co-op barometer – a weather clock.

Newcastle has a fine collection of unusual clocks and timepieces. The Keelmen's Hospital (1701) features sundials and a turret and clock which were added in 1772. There is a later sundial on the wall of Milburn House.

St Nicholas' Cathedral has had several clocks over the years. The first mention of a clock at St Nicholas' was in 1565, a clock with chimes was installed in 1761 and a new clock was erected in 1832 by John Walker. This clock was illuminated by gas light in 1833 causing

Clocks clockwise from the right: St Nicholas' Cathedral, the Guildhall, Northern Goldsmith's, Westgate Road, Keelmen's Hospital.

The clock on the Co-op, Newgate Street.

Exhibition Park.

great local excitement and inspiring a song called *The Fiery Clock-Fyce* by Robert Nunn. The current clock was rebuilt in 1885 by W. Potts of Leeds who still maintain the clock today.

Two of the city's best-known clocks are the Northern Goldsmiths' clocks in Blackett Street and Westgate Road. At the time of writing the clock in Westgate Road is under repair following an accident when the base of the clock fell to the ground narrowly missing a passer-by!

They were installed in 1935 at a cost of around £700 each, operated on a synchronome electrical impulse system, and were designed by Cackett, Burns Dick and Mackellar. The statue represents Venus, and fittingly the Blackett street clock was a popular meeting place for young lovers.

There's an Art Nouveau style clock on Emerson Chambers, while the Art Deco Co-operative store in Newgate Street has a clock face featuring the letters Co-operative on one tower and a barometer on the other. Their faces measure 8ft 6ins in diameter. The letter and numbers are neon and are illuminated at night.

The Coronation clock tower in Exhibition Park, erected in 1953, was a gift of the Freemen to the City of Newcastle. The tower is made of a special brick supplied by the National Coal Board and cost £757 6s 5d. Not far away is St Andrew's Churchyard in Jesmond which has a sexton's bell.

Thomas Yellowley

An architectural mystery: the 'Vampire Rabbit'

The 'Vampire Rabbit' in earlier colours. The mystery beast is now painted a fetching black.

Tucked away in the close behind Newcastle's St Nicholas' Cathedral hides one of the city's weirdest architectural features. Facing the back of the cathedral is an incongruously grand doorway at the rear of 27 Dean Street. The structure is very bulky and ornate: a mass of pink and cream Jacobean styling resembling a huge ormolu clock. Set above the doorway, surmounting the architrave, sits a large black-painted sculpture of a rabbit. The beast has unfeasibly large canine teeth, erect ears, and a manic expression on its face, which has led to it being nicknamed the 'Vampire Rabbit'.

Notwithstanding the inappropriately baroque grandeur of such a doorway in a back alley, the presence of the rabbit – a bizarre and alien presence in the cloistered tranquillity of a churchyard – has perplexed architectural historians for years. Why on earth is it there?

A closer look at the beast suggests it could well be a hare and this may provide a clue. In pre-Christian Europe, 'mad' March hares were associated with the advent of Spring. As Christianity became established, the hares were adopted as a representation of Easter in church iconography and architecture They also gave rise to the 'Easter bunny' along the way. Throughout Britain's medieval churches, there are examples of carved hares playing bagpipes; hares chasing Green men; and trios of hares in side-relief, running in circles, and sharing three ears arranged in such a way that each hare appears to have its own two ears – a so-called 'trinity of hares'. So sticking a hare, suitably enhanced in the grotesque tradition of gargoyles, above a back doorway may have been an aesthetic joke on the part of architects Oliver, Leeson and Wood, who designed the exuberant Cathedral Buildings office block for the Church Commissioners in 1901. Other buildings they designed in the city incorporate similar eye-catching features, such as the golden sunshine face that gazes up Neville Street from the Sun Insurance building.

The site suggests two other connections. The Cathedral Close was formerly the site of the workshop of engraver Thomas Bewick, whose work included many representations of wide-eyed hares. Moreover, the cathedral's patron saint, St. Nicholas of Myra, is closely associated in some East European Christmas stories with woodland animals such as hares and deer.

So no vampire rabbit after all? Maybe not, but it's certainly one of the finest pieces of post-medieval architectural detail on Tyneside.

Christopher Goulding

Stained glass

Glass from St Nicholas' Cathedral.

Newcastle has some fine examples of stained glass. Perhaps the oldest is in St John's Church, Westgate Road where some medieval fragments are roughly assembled in the north Chancel window. They include what is probably the earliest representation of the City Coat of Arms – the three castles.

Another piece of early pre-reformation glass is a beautiful roundel in St Nicholas' Cathedral depicting the Madonna feeding the Christ child; it is sometimes known as the 'First Supper'. While in St Nicholas' Cathedral, look out for a window memorial on the east wall in St George's Chapel. It commemorates Viscount Grey of Falloden who was foreign Secretary between 1905 and 1916 and was also founder of the Royal Society for the Protection of Birds. The window shows St Oswald holding a raven carrying a gold ring and attended by a dove with a halo, while St Cuthbert feeds finches from his hand and is attended by an eider duck. Another stained glass window in St George's

Chapel commemorates Charles Parsons; an angel above St Christopher is shown carrying *Turbinia*. In the nearby crypt, originally built as a charnel house, most of the windows depict industry except one which shows a lady and gentleman playing music.

The window in St Cuthbert's Chapel at St Nicholas' Cathedral depicts the Farne Islands and St Catherine's Hill, Winchester. Among the many birds and wildlife represented are the robin, puffin, tern, black-headed gull, mandarin duck, osprey and several squirrels and an otter. On the north wall is a representation of the *Mauretania* surrounded by the Blue Riband which she held for 22 years as the fastest liner crossing the North Atlantic. The window is a memorial to Andrew W. Laing who had interests in shipbuilding, energy and mining. Also featured in the window are American oil wells and local coalmining headstocks

St George's Church in Jesmond has window displaying an unusual clog calendar alphabet (medieval symbols which denote feast days) while in St Mary's Cathedral there is a window telling the story of the building of the Cathedral.

Down on the Side in the Crown Posada look out for some Pre-Raphaelite stained glass showing a Spanish looking gentlemen holding a glass of beer.

Thomas Yellowley

The secret bunker

The bunker at Kenton Bar has been an open secret for some time. Everyone seems to have heard about it. But how many know that it was the control centre for the Battle of Britain above Northern England, or that it was reused during the Cold War?

There's not much of the bunker visible above ground, but it's important to remember that it was just one part of a much larger Royal Air Force base, with accommodation, defensive pill-boxes and air-raid shelters, and even its own NAAFI. All of that was demolished when the Ministry of Agriculture moved in after 1948. There are just a few enigmatic concrete ventilators and radio aerial mast-bases on a large, flat-topped mound. The only buildings still there are the two entrances to the bunker; the larger one for the officers, and the smaller for other ranks. Both of these buildings are brick-fronted concrete with reinforced concrete roofs. The officer's entrance leads to a surprisingly flimsy wooden door with a rubber gas-tight seal, and then down a flight of stairs and a long corridor: to reduce the effects of blast, this dog-legs through ninety degrees, and ends in another gas-tight door. Corridors along either side of the bunker access a maze of rooms on two floors, including the plant room, which still has the original ventilation and filtration plant, and the operations room with its viewing galleries. The Ops Room floor has been removed, but the Ops Table is still stored in the bunker.

However, there are clues that the bunker has been used more recently. The instructions for the sewage ejector are pasted onto the reverse of an old RAF notice board. There are dormitories, something that wouldn't have been needed for an eight hour shift in 'the Hole', and it's clear that many of the internal rooms have been rearranged and the Ops table over-painted. These date from the Bunker's use by the Home Office as the Regional War Room for No 1 (Northern) Region as part of a network of Civil Defence Control Centres which would have been used in the event of nuclear war. But the biggest secret of all is that there was another bunker on the ministry site …

The damp emergency stairs from the lower level of the bunker.

❧ *John Mabbitt*

When I first came to work in the Lower Ouseburn I was struck by the scale of Byker Bridge and how it dwarfed the Ship Inn beneath it. That was eight years ago, and since then numerous people have said to me 'I've driven over Byker Bridge but never realized that so much was going on beneath it'.

Regeneration of the Lower Ouseburn has transformed an area once associated with heavy industry and hard labour into one of Newcastle's up and coming cultural destinations, noted for its real ale pubs, live music, artists' workshops and a centre for celebrating children's literature, Seven Stories.

Today Byker Bridge stands out against a soft green landscape of fields and trees, and the greenness of Ouseburn is another of its many attractions. Walking through the woodland, hearing so many birds calling to each other, makes the city centre seem like miles away rather than the few bus stops it actually is.

These trees and fields hide the scars of long gone industries. People lived alongside the Ouseburn as recently as the 1940s in housing that

Between Byker Bridge and the railway viaduct, 1935.

dated from the previous century with no electricity and a water supply that more often than not was a stand-pipe in a common yard. I have been fortunate enough to meet some of them. A frequent comment is that 'we may have been poor but we all knew each other'.

You can't go anywhere in the Lower Ouseburn without discovering some detail of the area's past. Stepney Bank Stables might be the city's only indoor riding arena but it is also a precious link with the heritage of horse-drawn haulage; its 1870s stable-yard still in use much as it was when first built.

❧ Mike Greatbatch

The hidden bridge over a hidden river

The arch of the old High Bridge photographed during an excavation beneath Grey Street.

High Bridge, between Pilgrim Street and the Bigg Market is so interesting because it is one of the many Tyneside bridges that aren't bridges any more. It was originally the site of Overdene Brigg, the medieval crossing over the Lort Burn. Others include Barras Bridge; Stockbridge, just off the Quayside; and Low Bridge, just below the Cathedral and New Bridge Street. These lost bridges show just how far the peo-

ple of Newcastle have altered the whole landscape of their town; in places the backfill of the Pandon is over 12 metres deep; Grainger's backfilling of the Lort Burn for Grey Street is thought to be around eight metres deep.

To understand why the city centre of Newcastle is laid out in the way that it is now, you have to understand its rivers, particularly the small rivers and burns which flow down into the Tyne. In medieval times, the Lort Burn divided the town in two, flowing between the market streets and Pilgrim Street. It could only be crossed in two places, which became important routes providing the only east to west links between the major streets of the town.

Walking down High Bridge, it's easy to get an idea of what Newcastle looked like before Grainger reshaped the town centre. Compared with Grainger's Shakespeare Street, High Bridge is much narrower and the buildings on either side simply aren't as uniform. Rather than being a big planned development, the land was sold or let bit by bit from the back plot of the buildings fronting onto Pilgrim Street, as the landowners realised that land with a street frontage was precious to anyone with a business or shop. While the vast majority of the buildings on High Bridge are Victorian or later, their frontages preserve the irregular sizes of plots which come from the piecemeal development of this part of town.

High Bridge isn't just important as an interesting oddity – the bridge that isn't there any more, but as an example of how the medieval town layout can survive in a city centre that was almost completely rebuilt in the nineteenth century. Even though the Lort Burn has long been culverted, High Bridge remains one of the most important routes across the town. And that all stems from it having once been a bridge.

Oliver's map of 1830 shows the line of the Lort Burn below High Bridge before Grey Street was built.

❧ *John Mabbitt*

Seahorses – proper, crined and finned

Mansion House

Lynn Pearson

Newcastle is a super city for seahorse spotting. The city's coat of arms sports a mythical pair of them as supporters, their appearance described heraldically as 'proper, crined and finned or', that is in natural colours with gold manes, fins and tails. For a real seahorse, however, natural is mostly transparent, unlike the very solid stone couple found squashed into the pediment of the former 1860s bank on the corner of Westgate Road and Grainger Street. They are lying down ('couchant'), their webbed hooves barely visible. Another pair, dating from 1892, look across at the Monument from 22 Blackett Street, where they balance on their tails while supporting a dormer window. Round in Northumberland Street, on the wall of the broad passageway which rises towards Eldon Square, is a sad seahorse, all alone, clearly the left (and left behind) of a pair from the city's arms on a building torn down to make way for the shopping centre. Also alone, but rather more perky, is a larger-than-life modernist concrete specimen in Northumberland Road; equipped with a trident, this seahorse plays its part in a 1974 mural depicting 'Newcastle Through the Ages'.

The most superlative seahorses are to be seen at the Civic Centre (1960-8), their natural home in the city. Here are superabundant seahorses in wood, glass, metal and even tapestry. Most intriguing is their presence on two pendant light fittings suspended in the spacious Grand Stair Hall is an 11-tier crystal chandelier, with four perfect crystal seahorses (looking almost as they would in the ocean) at its lowest point, while the East Staircase light fitting has a double ring of symbolic metal seahorses, each emanating from a tiny version of the city's shield.

The seahorse heads at Newcastle Civic Centre, September 1967.

But nothing can match the 12 massive bronze seahorse heads which top the Civic Centre's carillon tower, looking down serenely – or is that

menacingly? – on the city. At their largest, a real seagoing seahorse can be just over a foot long, so if we could see the whole of these incredible, identical bronze beasts, they would each be more than 20 feet high. They were designed by John Robert Murray McCheyne (1911-82), then Master of Sculpture at King's College, which became the University of Newcastle upon Tyne in 1963. Mysterious and magnificent, these monsters are the most memorable seahorses in the world, let alone the city.

❧ *Lynn Pearson*

TRIUMPHANS

Seahorses in stone, wood and bronze.
Clockwise from above: a newel post at
the Mansion House; the carillon at the
Civic Centre; the City Crest; on a pillar
at St Nicholas' Cemetery, Fenham.

FORTITER TRIUMPHANS
DEFENDIT

201

Above, Newcastle's Free Library around 1890. A resolution to open a free library in the town was first passed by the council in 1854 but it was not until 1882 that the library in New Bridge Street was opened.

In 1968 that building was replaced by Sir Basil Spence's library, right, and in 2009 a new City Library will open on the same spot.

Mark Thurston

An impression of the new City Library by Kajima Partnerships Ltd.

And finally …

It is a real pleasure to be asked to contribute to this gem of a book. Of course I'm going to use the opportunity to comment on libraries. There is a fine and long-established tradition of public libraries throughout Tyneside. They all provide a wide range of high quality services.

As Newcastle's City Librarian I realise I may be biased, but I really would like to single out Newcastle's Local and Family History Services as one of the most significant in the region and beyond. The collection contains unique resources which are part of the city's heritage, such as the published works and engraving tools of Thomas Bewick, Gibsone's conches (exquisite drawings of shells), Dr Thomlinson's Library (the first ever 'public library collection' in Newcastle), and Charles Avison's original scores. Add to them our unrivalled collections of local maps, books, newspapers and illustrations, as well as contemporary press cuttings, records, cassettes, CDs, videos, DVDs and digital media, and it's clear that we have an enormous treasure-box of information about Newcastle and the wider region, its history and its people.

For well over 100 years, librarians and other collectors in Newcastle have worked hard to source, acquire and make accessible a unique local and family history resource. This service – this collection –- has always been a foundation of Newcastle's Library Service. It has been developed with the interested resident, the school pupil, the family historian, the published writer, and the academic researcher all equally in mind.

In 2006 Newcastle's Library Service is poised to begin the dramatic move towards a 21st century building and the new library will be the backdrop, the display case, to these truly wonderful and unique resources.

With the acknowledged bias of a City Librarian, I am convinced that Newcastle's Local and Family History Library is the finest on Tyneside. And with what we have planned for our new City Library, it will become even finer.

Tony Durcan

Contributors and selected publications

(Those published by Tyne Bridge Publishing are identified TBP; OP denotes out of print. Visit www.tynebridgepublishing.co.uk for all our current books.)

Max Adams, historian, writer and broadcaster, author of *Collingwood, Northumberland's Heart of Oak* (TBP, 2005); *Collingwood, Nelson's Own Hero* (Weidenfeld, 2005).

Ian Ayris, Historic Environment Manager, Newcastle City Council, author of *A City of Palaces: Richard Grainger …* (TBP 1997); co-author of *On the Waterfront* (TBP 1998 OP).

Brian Bennison, social historian and writer, author of *A History of Newcastle's Public Houses: Heady Days* (TBP 1996 OP); *Heavy Nights* (TBP 1997); *Lost Weekends* (TBP 1998).

Janis Blower, feature writer, *The Shields Gazette*, author of *All Together Like the Folk o' Shields* (Northeast Press).

Maureen Brook, teacher and writer, author of *Herring Girls and Hiring Fairs* (TBP 2005).

Douglas Bond, local historian, co-author of *Victorian and Edwardian Northumberland* (Batsford, 1976).

Dr Maureen Callcott, historian and writer.

Agnes Chilton, writer.

Alex Croom, Curator, Arbeia Roman Fort and Museum, Tyne & Wear Museums.

John Dobson, maritime historian.

Tony Durcan, Head of Culture, Libraries & Lifelong Learning, Newcastle City Council.

Dr Constance Fraser, historian, antiquarian and writer, co-author of *Northumbria* (Phillimore, 1989); (ed) *Newcastle Chamberlains Accounts 1508-1511*.

Ron French, maritime historian and writer, co-author of *Lost Shipyards of the Tyne* (TBP 2004).

Christopher Goulding, schoolteacher and writer, author of *Hidden Newcastle* (TBP 1994 OP) and Tinseltoon (TBP 1998).

Douglas Glendinning, art historian and writer, author of *The Art of Mining* (TBP 2000 OP); co-author of *Thomas Bewick* (TBP 2003).

Mike Greatbatch, Heritage and Interpretation Development Officer, Newcastle City Council.

John Grundy, historian, writer and broadcaster, author of, *Townscape* (Northern Heritage, 1990); *Northern Pride* (Granada, 2003); and co author of 2nd edition of Pevsner's *Northumberland* (Yale, 1992).

Marshall Hall, art historian and writer, author of *The Artists of Northumbria* (Art Dictionaries Ltd, 2005).

Tony Henderson, Environment Editor, *The Journal*, Newcastle, author of *My Country, Discovering North East England* (First Edition, 2005).

David Heslop, Tyne and Wear County Archaeologist, co-author of *Alderman Fenwick's House* (Society of Antiquaries, 2001).

Thomas Hewitson, military historian and writer, author of *A Soldier's Life* (TBP 1999 OP); *Weekend Warriors: from Tyne to Tweed* (Tempus, 2006).

David Hughes, Friend of the Avison Ensemble.

Ian Jackson, Secretary Durham and North East Branch, Cricket Society.

Richard E. Keys, maritime historian and writer, co-author of *Tales from the Tyne* (TBP 2006); *Tall Ships on the Tyne* (TBP 2005); *A Dictionary of Tyne Sailing Ships*.

Anthea Lang, Local History Librarian, Gateshead Council.

Jack and John Leslie, local historians and writers, co-authors of *Down Our Streets: Newcastle Street Names Explored* (TBP 2003).

Tony Liddell, archaeologist, ghost investigator and writer, author of *Otherworld North East* (TBP 2004).

Dr Stafford M. Linsley, industrial archaeologist, author of *Ports and Harbours of Northumberland* (Tempus 2005); *Spanning the Tyne* (TBP 1998 OP).

David Lovie, historian, writer and heritage consultant, author of *Buildings of Grainger Town*, Millennium Edition (Grainger Town Partnership, 2001); *The Cathedral Church of St Nicholas, Newcastle, Guidebook*.

Grace McCombie, buildings historian and writer, co-author of 2nd edition of Pevsner's *Northumberland* (Yale, 1992).

Professor Norman McCord, historian and writer, author of *British History 1815-1906* (OUP, 1991); *The Northern Counties from AD 1000* (Longman, 1998) and many others.

John Mabbitt, Assistant Keeper of Field Archaeology, Tyne & Wear Museums.

Frank Manders, local historian, cinema historian and writer, author of *Cinemas of Newcastle* (TBP 2005); co-author of *Crossing the Tyne* (TBP 2001).

Steve Mayes, photographer, author of *Newcastle-Gateshead in Black and White* (TBP 2004).

Readers at Newcastle Central Library around 1910.

Alan Morgan, City Guide, local historian and writer, author of *Beyond the Grave* (TBP 2004); *A Fine and Private Place* (TBP 2000).

Adrian Osler, maritime historian, author of *Mr Greathead's Lifeboats* (T&WM).

Lynn Pearson, architectural historian, photographer and writer, author of *Public Art Since 1950* (Shire, 2006); *Famous Graves* (Shire, 2004); *Northern City* (TBP 1996 OP) and many others.

Archie Potts, social and sports historian and writer, author of *Zilliacus: A Life for Peace and Socialism* (Merlin Press, 2002).

Richard Potts, archivist and writer, co-author of *Crossing the Tyne* (TBP 2001); *Dame Sarah's Legacy: A History of the Lady Hewley Trust* (Hewley Trust, 2005).

Barry Redfern, retired police officer historian and writer; author of *The Shadow of the Gallows* (TBP 2003); *Victorian Villains: Prisoners from Newcastle Gaol 1871-1873* (TBP 2006).

Liz Rees, Chief Archivist, Tyne & Wear Archives Service.

Robert W. Rennison, civil engineer and historian, author of *Water to Tyneside* (Newcastle, Gateshead Water Co., 1979); *Civil Engineering Heritage: Northern England* (1996).

Denise Robertson, broadcaster.

Ken Smith, maritime historian, writer and sub-editor, *The Journal*, Newcastle, author of *Emperor of Industry: Lord Armstrong of Cragside* (TBP 2005); *Mauretania* (TBP, 1997); *Turbinia* (TBP, 1996); *Stephenson Power* (TBP 2003); co-author of *Swan Hunter, the Pride and the Tears* (TBP 2005); *Lost Shipyards of the Tyne* (TBP 2004); *Tall Ships on the Tyne* (TBP 2005); *Tales from the Tyne* (TBP 2006).

Barbara Stephenson, food historian and writer, author of *With a Northumbrian Flavour* (TBP 1992 OP).

Nigel Todd, political and social historian and City Councillor, author of *The Militant Democracy, Joseph Cowen and Victorian Radicalism* (Bewick Press, 1991); *In Excited Times: the People Against the Blackshirts* (Bewick Press, 1994).

Jenny Uglow, historian, writer, author of *A Little History of British Gardening* (Chatto, 2004); *The Lunar Men* (Faber, 2003); *Nature's Engraver: a Life of Thomas Bewick* (Faber, 2006), and many others.

Paul Wappat, broadcaster.

Hildred Whale, Information and Education Coordinator, South Tyneside Libraries.

David Whetstone, Culture Editor, *The Journal*, Newcastle.

Ian Whitehead, Keeper of Maritime History, Tyne & Wear Museums, author of *James Renforth of Gateshead, Champion Sculler of the World* (TBP 2004); *The Sporting Tyne, a History of Professional Rowing* (T&WM).

Ian Wilson, writer and sub-editor, *The Evening Chronicle*, Newcastle.

Dr Thomas Yellowley, local historian and photographer.

Michael Young, local historian, walker and writer.

Selective index to places, people and ships mentioned in the text

Ships